Dr. Mary's Church
Waddington, NY

A MANUAL
FOR
CHURCH
MUSICIANS

A MANUAL
FOR
CHURCH
MUSICIANS

PREFACE BY

Paul J. Hallinan
Archbishop of Atlanta

THE LITURGICAL CONFERENCE / *Washington, D.C.*

The Liturgical Conference
2900 Newton Street, N.E.
Washington, D.C.   20018

Library of Congress Catalog Card Number 64-8257

A MANUAL FOR CHURCH MUSICIANS *is a publication in
the* Parish Worship Program, *a Liturgical Conference Project*

PRINTED IN THE UNITED STATES OF AMERICA BY
GARAMOND/PRIDEMARK PRESS, BALTIMORE, MARYLAND

PREFACE

The point of this small book is not just to get better music in the Church. It is more complex than that. We are seeking today to put better music in the context of better prayer. Renovation of the ways of Christian worship demands music worthy of the praying, participating people of God.

An outspoken American Catholic bishop of the 1880's, Richard Gilmour, once surprised a national meeting of church musicians by telling them:

> The Methodists started out with a clear, distinct shout. It was spoken of as a "Methodist shout." But it was a shout that sought for the people, and it said to the people: "Shout with us! Sing with us!"

Gilmour, a convert from Protestantism, added: "It is a grand thing to get the cobwebs out of the throat, and it helps a great deal to get the cobwebs out of the soul."

But people in church will not sing without an invitation and an encouragement. The history of sacred music has gone up and down the arpeggio of sentimentality, sensuousness and suffocation, spaced with long bars of silence by the congregation. Now we are ending such a silent period. In the spirit of the new *Constitution on the Sacred Liturgy* we are responding to St. Paul's plea that we be filled with the Spirit, "speaking to one another in psalms, hymns and spiritual songs, singing and making melody in your hearts to the Lord."

7

The Fathers of the Second Vatican Council, in the articles on Sacred Music, mention the active participation of the people six times. Choirs, of course, are to be diligently promoted, but the whole body of the faithful must be able to take their rightful part. Gregorian Chant is especially suited to the Roman liturgy, but an edition of simpler chants is needed. Polyphony has its place, if it is in accord with the liturgical spirit, but nothing is to prevent that "the voices of the faithful may ring out."

The Council Fathers are simply carrying on the tradition of the early Fathers of the Church. Ephrem the Deacon asked, "Do you know what a hymn is? It is song with praise of God." Basil and John Chrysostom found in sacred music a "gentle deception" on the part of God: to teach and encourage men by the words while they were being charmed by the melody and rhythm. Augustine thought that the real piety of the psalms came through (to use a current phrase) in a more holy way when sung than when only read.

How did we lose this truly Catholic experience? There is a clue in the popular notion that sacred music was meant to be heard and admired by the prayerful, rather than really performed by men at prayer. In a century noted for fine operatic music, for example, the song of the Church imitated opera. In our times, with their familiar veneer of sentimentality, our congregations have been reared on hymns that combined cheap tunes and feeble theology. That both the great music of the stage and the bad music of banality are out of place in the worship of God is becoming clear to a discerning generation. What we are going to do about it is not so evident.

This book points the way. If properly used, it will encourage the people to sing out, and to sing as well as the voice God gave them permits. It can do more. It can double the value of the traditional choir. To its duty of singing the more unusual parts, it can add the golden opportunity of encouraging the whole congregation in its own parts. Composers will be enheartened to write good Mass melodies and hymns for popular use. Directors will find the new dimension of congregational music a higher challenge.

When the first high Mass in English was sung in St. Louis August 27, 1964, Dr. C. A. Peloquin composed the music. A newspaper music critic, calling it "powerful" and "dramatic," analyzed it in terms of "the broadened horizons of the music world of the Catholic Church." He warned musicians against diluting the high standard of beauty in Catholic Church music. In this, he was in agreement with Augustine that bad singing is pleasing to neither God nor man. In composing, directing and singing the praise of God, there can be no excuse for mediocrity.

Even when a congregation is small or not fully trained, full and hearty participation in music suited to this purpose need never be mediocre. Indeed when well done out of a deeper "delight" in praise of God, and as a manifestation of "unity of minds," in the language of the *Constitution*, popular sacred song can prove to be the threshhold of the great music demanded by its theme. This book can lead us to that threshhold.

☦ PAUL J. HALLINAN
Archbishop of Atlanta

ACKNOWLEDGMENTS

The Liturgical Conference wishes to acknowledge gratefully the help of the following, who contributed their knowledge and experience to this volume: Rev. William Bauman, Diocesan Director of Music, Kansas City, Mo.; Dr. Clifford Bennett, President, The Gregorian Institute of America, Cleveland, Ohio; Rev. Lawrence Brett, Diocesan Liturgical Commission, Springdale, Conn.; Rev. William Crowley, St. Francis de Sales High School, Chicago, Illinois; Rev. Cletus Madsen, St. Ambrose College, Davenport, Iowa; Rev. Clement J. McNaspy, S.J., Music Editor, *America* Magazine, New York, New York; Mother Josephine Morgan, R.S.C.J., Pius X School of Liturgical Music, Manhattanville College of the Sacred Heart, Purchase, New York; Rev. Eugene A. Walsh, S.S., Archdiocesan Liturgical Commission, Professor of Music, St. Mary's Seminary, Baltimore, Md.; Mr. Omer Westendorf, President, World Library of Sacred Music, Cincinnati, Ohio.

CONTENTS

INTRODUCTION

The birth of the Lord was announced in song, and the last thing that Jesus did with his disciples before his death was to join with them in the singing of a hymn. The life that Christ now lives within his Church is also rounded out with singing, for Christian tradition has seen fit to accord a prominent place of honor to music within the sacred liturgy, and especially in the liturgical sacrifice which proclaims that same death of the Lord until he comes again.

Moreover, it may be noted that the message of the birth of the Savior was given to shepherds; it came to them in words they could readily understand, and they, in turn, were moved to glorify and praise God "for all that they had *heard* and seen." Similarly, the familiar Hallel Psalms that brought the Last Supper to a close were sung by the very men who would be the first shepherds of the flock of Christ, and took place just prior to the Master's warning that they would lose heart and scatter like sheep when he, the great Shepherd, would be struck down.

In these days of liturgical renewal, God has once again seen fit to give to shepherds a prominent role in the task of making his praise resound from the lips of his people in their own tongues and with sacred melody. In the first place, it was the late Pope John the Good who, motivated by a deep pastoral concern, was responsible for the great undertaking of the *aggiornamento* of the Church. Following the example of Pope John, and with the same spirit of enthusi-

13

asm, the shepherds of the universal flock have made this "bringing-up-to-date" of the Church their primary concern. The Constitution on the Sacred Liturgy is the first-fruits of their labor, and for this one fact alone we shall ever be indebted to them.

The Role of the American Bishops

It is to the shepherds of the American Church, however, that we owe the greater burden of our gratitude, and this for several reasons. First, their decision to make use of the vernacular concessions is an indication of how clearly the American episcopate has grasped the pastoral nature of the Ecumenical Council in general, and of Chapter One on the Sacred Liturgy in particular. It is a tribute to their incisiveness that, despite the promulgation of the liturgical decrees under the guise of law, they have nevertheless come to recognize the principles set forth in those decrees as being matters of truth and doctrine with which they are desirous of nourishing the people entrusted to their care.

Secondly, they were generous in their allowance for the use of English in the Mass and Sacraments, a generosity that is not only a reflection and reaffirmation of the Constitution, but its continuation as well. Lastly, and most fittingly for our purposes of consideration, they acted forcefully and with daring to assure the equal application of the vernacular to the sung rites. This last fact is all the more impressive when one considers the difficulties that lie ahead, difficulties that were fully recognized as such, and which will provide a challenge to liturgists and musicians alike. In the light of the obstacles that will stand in the way of making the sung English Mass a living, purposeful, and yet beautiful activity of the Christian community, many might be tempted to hesitate in moving forward, and prefer to stand still. Conceivably, not a few might even wish to take refuge in the past, apprehensive lest the great contributions of renowned masters in the field of Church music be lost to sight.

Yet it is just such an attitude of temerity that the bishops of the Church in America have avoided, and with rare insight have grasped the fundamental principle of all science (and certainly the study of ecclesiastical music must be so classified), namely that discovery can only come after experimentation. In the light of the future restoration and restructuring of the liturgy, a certain experimentation is necessary and even desired. To postpone the inevitable period of trial and adjustment until such time as a revised rite is available would be disastrous. It is not in spite of the risks, but because of them, that the bishops of the United States have decreed the equal application of the "greater use of the mother tongue" to sung Masses.

Such a provision will allow ample time for trial and probation, but has wider practical advantages as well. Where there are many sung Masses during the week, the people would be deprived of a vernacular liturgy were Latin to be maintained for the music of the Mass, and it is well argued that the popularity of Sunday low Masses in English would out-rival the High Mass in Latin. Furthermore, a unity between dialogue and sung Masses would be maintained, thus avoiding undue confusion on the part of the people. It is certainly not a question of "participation at any and all costs," but participation at some costs cannot be avoided. As many astute observers of human nature have indicated, there will be some people who would prefer the "familiar incomprehensible" to the "unfamiliar comprehensible," and it would be unnatural not to expect the coming changes to alienate some. Here it must be borne in mind, however, that the estrangement will only be in the nature of a prelude, and that all chords, even the discordant, come to rest.

The Contribution of Church Musicians

If we can rejoice at the bold decisions of the American hierarchy to strive to achieve a meaningful and expressive pattern of worship regardless of the seemingly insurmountable difficulties, we can do so only because of the work of historians and liturgists whose depth of study has revealed the true relationship between music and liturgy. To pass over the achievements of the musicians of the past would be to fail in our understanding of the basic fact that music has always served the liturgy as its handmaid. Within this relationship, both become vital instruments in the work of redemption; apart from this relationship there can only arise a false sense of values that leads to misunderstanding and disharmony.

No less a master of the history of ecclesiastical music than Karl Fellerer (cf. bibliography) has pointed out that a polarity exists between music and liturgy, nor has anyone been as successful as he in indicating that such a state of tension must of necessity exist. It would be as unrealistic to deny this truth as it would be to deny that tension exists within the hair-spring of a watch; but it is a tension that is causative of movement and measure. Throughout the course of the history of the Church, this polarity is seen to be at work, with the emphasis now upon liturgy, now upon music, and with the great ages of creativity and aesthetic beauty coming at those times when a balance between the two came into being.

The great difficulty in the course of this recurring fluctuation, is that music is an autonomous science, governed by laws that lie beyond the scope of liturgical discipline, whereas liturgy restricts and narrows the freedom of any science employed in her service. Liturgy goes beyond the personal, of which music is fond, to give expression to the communal, and is Godward in its direction of giving delight, not manward.

Music seeks to express itself with free and unimpeded use of its own laws and formulae, whereas liturgy searches out the functional aspects of music in order to use it in the sacred work which is the worship of God. This was especially true as the art of music developed outside the sphere of church music, where it is rightly a mistress among the other arts. The scope of freedom that music enjoyed among peoples generally could not but exert a profound influence upon the strictly liturgical usage of music by the People of God. As time and the development of varied forms of music continued, three distinct stages of liturgical music can be noted.

The first, and earliest, is the instinctive use of music as a means of expressing truly Christian sentiments; it arose from within the structure of the liturgy, and was determined by its format. Priest, people, and eventually choirs, had specific functions to perform—their own specific "liturgies." This was the age of music *of* the liturgy. It gave rise to the development of the plain chant, rooted in the melodies of the Eastern and Mediterranean regions, yet proving itself the perfect vessel of expression for the Latin language when, after a lengthy period of experimentation, this vernacular became familiar to a people used to Greek in the liturgy.

Only after Church music became an independent art and encouraged the development of the free style and polyphony does a rift appear between liturgy and music. This led to the formation of music *for* the liturgy. With the further decline in understanding of what the liturgy is, we arrive at the last, and saddest, state of music *at* the liturgy. The development of the so-called "private Masses," where the priest assumed the roles previously enjoyed by choir and people, hastened this latter course of events, one that has persisted to the present days, and which the recent pontiffs have been so zealous to change.

To the musicians who did their utmost to achieve a sense of refinement and restraint in the composition of music *for* the liturgy, we owe no small measure of indebtedness. In their approximation to the spirit of the plain chant, they preserved a notion of what liturgical music should be, and this in spite of the fact that awareness of the liturgy was at low ebb. To the musicians of the recent past we owe much of the interest that has led to the present renewal of the Church's life of prayer. Their invaluable love for the ideals of the chant guided the *Motu Proprio* of Pope Pius X, and made the Church conscious of her musical heritage. One recalls Johann Ett, and his essay at simplifying the melodic line; Franz Xavier Witt, and the organization of the Caecilian Society; Dom Gueranger of Solesmes, Dom Jausion and Dom Pothier, among others.

They took an important step in directing the study of music as being *for* the liturgy, and endowed the composers and musicians with the privileged task of leading the Church forward to an understanding of music as being *of* the liturgy; their task has been clearly enunciated by the fathers of the present Ecumenical Council:

> Liturgical worship is given a more noble form when the divine offices are celebrated solemnly in song, with the assistance of sacred ministers and the active participation of the people (Constitution, Art. 113).
>
> Religious singing by the people is to be skillfully fostered, so that in devotions and sacred exercises, as also during liturgical services, the voices of the faithful may ring out according to the norms and requirements of the rubrics (Constitution, Art. 118).

Musicians have the role of working with the "bishops and other pastors of souls" to "be at pains to ensure that, whenever the sacred action is to be celebrated with song, the whole body of the faithful may be able to contribute that active participation which is rightly theirs" (Constitution, Art. 114). As in the many papal pronouncements which preceded, and prepared for, the present legislation of Vatican II, polyphony and suitable modern music are recognized as being of great use for the purpose of worship; as always, "pride of place" is given to the Gregorian chant, with the accompanying phrase "other things being equal." This reference to the vernacular concessions, so phrased as to respect the sensibilities of those who love the chant and acknowledge the wedding of words and music, is of particular importance. Despite its apparent insignificance, this short phrase underlines the eminently pastoral concern of the present Constitution, which is above all else, a reaffirmation of the mind of the Church.

The Pastoral Concern of the Church

Although the plain chant is one of the priceless treasures, it is primarily the domain of the monastery; it has never been the actual treasure of the American parish. Our priests were "exposed" to it during the formative years of the seminary training, and occasionally a hard-working choirmaster has introduced it, but not without hard effort and even some opposition. There is no need to fear that the chant will be lost, for the monastery will preserve it, whereas the parish never really possessed it. For the monk, Latin will not prove a barrier to his understanding of the Church's ceremonial; for the average parishioner, English will prove an invitation to an understanding of the worship of the Whole Christ that Latin could never give. It is the parish that is the first concern of the bishops, and intelligent participation the motive that underlies their liberal allowance for the use of English.

It is clearly the mind of the Church, reaffirmed by the decree of the American bishops, that Christ's faithful be led to share fully in Catholic worship, and especially in the sung rites which more closely approximate the heavenly liturgy. The whole emphasis of the present is upon the pastoral needs of the Church, and upon the nature of her worship as communal. The liturgy is viewed as the celebration of the mystery of our redemption, and the source of a vigorous Christian life formed by that worship. Since the didactic aspects of the liturgy have been highlighted, intelligibility has received the greatest attention. Until the principle of an intelligent and instructful worship is restored to the Church, the other characteristics of the liturgy must recede temporarily, until a balance between understanding and aesthetic perception is gained. Such an abeyance, should it come about, would be a negligible and necessary sacrifice; it need not come about if liturgists and musicians are motivated by the same pastoral concern that animated the deliberations of the Fathers of the Council.

Briefly, one can say that the mind of the Church is summed up in the very purposes of the Council set forth in the introduction of the Constitution on the Sacred Liturgy.

"To impart an ever increasing vigor to the Christian life of the faithful." Here the core of the matter is presented— the renewal of the innermost life of the Church, which begins with the renewal of the very source and center of the truly Christian spirit. Not change alone, nor change for the sake of change, but an attempt to bring about a "change of heart," a cleansing of the minds and hearts of Christ's own people by means of the waters of the Spirit that flow upon the Church through the designs and deliberations of her shepherds.

"To adapt more suitably to the needs of our own times those institutions that are subject to change"—a principle that has governed the activity of the Church throughout the course of her sojourn upon earth, one thoroughly in keeping with the pastoral interests of the bishops, and rooted in the incontrovertible fact that the timelessness of the Gospel must be accepted by men conditioned by time and place.

"To foster whatever can promote union among all who believe in Christ." The ecumenical aim of the Ecumenical Council. Certainly a liturgy in the language of the people will do much to increase the bonds that unite all those who "believe in Christ," many of whom worship the God and Father of our Lord in forms derived from the Mass. The communions of the Reformation claim the restoration of the

Mass to the people, and have offered possible solutions in their liturgies to the problem of how the present-day musician can work to achieve a beautiful and popular liturgy.

"To strengthen whatever can help to call the whole of mankind into the household of the Church." This last of the four aims seeks to announce the message of salvation to the whole world; the liturgy strives to announce this same message to the household of the faith, so that it may take deeper root. It can do this only with a worship that is intelligent, reverent, and impressive. The first of these adjectives belongs to the translators; the second, to the revisers of the liturgy; the third, to the musicians. Yet all three apply equally to each endeavor.

This, then, is the mind of the Church, for which the Church sees "particularly cogent reasons for undertaking the reform and promotion of the liturgy" (Constitution, Art. 1). Immediately after setting forth the guiding principles of the proposed reform, the Constitution is careful to place the whole of the work within the context of the diocese and the parish, (Articles 41 and 42), with insistence upon the practical fostering of the "liturgical life of the parish."

Since a considerable role is given to sacred music in the promotion of the liturgical spirit, this manual is written to discuss the implications of the forthcoming vernacular liturgy, and to treat of the role of the musician in bringing about a full, active participation by all the faithful in the mysteries of Christ. Forming, as it does, a "necessary or integral part of the solemn liturgy," particular emphasis is laid upon the precisely "ministerial function supplied by sacred music in the service of the Lord" (Constitution, Art. 112).

CHAPTER ONE

MUSIC AND WORSHIP

At a time when the entire world is undergoing a period of transition, the Church is found to be actively engaged in the same work—a revision of all the elements of her ordered life, notably the deepest aspect, her public worship. Such a task of restructuring will have a tremendous impact upon the Church musician. He has already seen many changes within the field of music, witnessed the work of modern composers, such as Poulenc and Britten, in bringing music to larger groups of people without sacrificing aesthetic and technical standards, and has become acquainted with new approaches to melody, rhythm, tone color, etc. Now he must face the great work of restoring to music her rightful role in the liturgy of the Church, a problem that is brought into sharper focus when one considers the sense of urgency attending the revision of the patterns of public prayer.

And yet, if the ordinary parish is to be affected by, and effective in, living the liturgy, the Church musician emerges as the person who will be the greatest aid in encouraging the active participation of the faithful. His professional services are sorely needed by the Church, perhaps more so now than at any other time in her history. The Church musician (and by this we mean not only composers and students of musical theory, but organists, choirmasters and singers as well) is given a challenge, one that involves his every talent and desire.

The Role of Music in Worship

Simply stated, music is a servant in the house of the Lord, to serve whom is to reign. This is the basic principle underlying any and all relationships between liturgy and music. Although music enjoys the primacy among the finer arts, it acquires an even higher prominence because of its intimate connection with the sacred rites, of which it is an *integral part*. The liturgy, after all, is a celebration, and a celebration without music is alien to human experience. The plastic arts have never occupied this central position, for, unlike sculpture or architecture, music clothes the Word of God itself, gives it a more intensive expression and heightens our reception of that creative Word. Although music is superior to the other arts in general, it is even more so in the liturgy, but only to the degree that it is willing to adapt itself to the needs of cult, and to be circumscribed by its demands. By this extramusical limitation, Church music is distinguished from purely secular music, and from religious music (which does give expression to religious sentiments, but apart from its use in the liturgy).

In its development as an art, liturgical music can never seek to free itself from the inner limitations imposed upon it by liturgical practicality, for otherwise it tends to become merely ornamental, irrelevant and external to worship, and even at variance with the very spirit of worship. In its development as an art at the service of the Church, music provides the proper setting for the liturgy, and to the point where it is capable of deepening the liturgical experience of the faithful, and of expressing their common faith, it renders itself truly genuine and necessary. The ability of any art to place itself within the perspective of usefulness and assignation broadens its artistic character; for music, the ultimate aim is to offer to God a tribute that is no less beautiful for being functional, one in which the song of priest, people and choir forms a unity.

The Musical Tradition of the Church

In the necessary work of restoration of the liturgy, the tradition of the Church must be the well-spring of inspiration and endeavor, but the return to former methods must never be considered more important than the future reform. This holds true for the liturgist as for the musicologist. Past traditions are often approached in the wrong way, with one's pre-conceived notions of what *should have been* determining the interpretation of facts.

Two extremes are to be avoided: the first is that of antiquarianism, a restoration of what was done before because of a love for a certain era of history, with the attending danger of choosing the wrong age, one in which things were done at variance with the liturgical spirit; the second danger is that of exaggerated adaptation, in which past poor performance causes a reaction against all past performance, and new, ephemeral elements are introduced. In determining the tradition of Church music, no easy interpretation is available. What is the traditional role of music? Why was it allowed to change so radically? Which age best represents that tradition?

The questions could continue, and could only be answered

by the historian of music, but in general there are certain recurring elements throughout the course of liturgical development that permit us to state, rather sketchily, that the traditions of the Church are contained in the papal directives of the past sixty years. At the same time, we are forced to admit that the present Constitution, while continuing these traditions, has undertaken the task of creating new and authentic tradition in the light of past greatness and present need.

That tradition points to Gregorian chant as the perfect model of liturgical music in the Roman liturgy, honors polyphony as worthy of the Church, especially as it approximates the chant, and allows for modern music to be used; furthermore, it places Church music *within* the context of the liturgy, which is seen to be communal and hierarchic, pastoral and didactic. All of these elements are distilled and refined, and made the essence of the Constitution's direction.

From each age of Church music, certain principles emerge that have shaped the course of events, and which should serve as suitable guides for the present time of transition. From the primitive age we may draw the principle that the purpose of music is to enhance the words, to give them a new, deeper meaning not given them by mere recitation. The origins of Church music point to the ceremonial chant of the synagogue, with its chanting of the Scriptures aloud and in unison, emphasising key words by raising the pitch, and rounding out each sentence by lowering the voice a tone or two.

From the age of the chant, the simplicity and ease of singing are seen as guiding norms; the people were never denied their part, while full use of the musical idiom was encouraged, especially by the cantors and choir. But from a music which was intended for the use of all, there developed a partition according to proper function. The further development of music that witnessed the richness of polyphony gave the Church the tradition of embellishment and the gift of highly developed skills by composers and singers alike. These three stages of primitive, plain song and polyphonic music follow the growth of the liturgy, and establish the traditions of liturgical music: it is ancillary to the text, allowing for the people to take their rightful part as worshippers; it has an important role in its own right, and is ordered to the hierarchic as well as to the communal, thus giving each "office" its musical assignment; it adds to the dignity and solemnity of the rites in a way that unison singing cannot, although it may never assume the place of common sung prayer.

These traditions, like the liturgical traditions to which they are inseparably joined, are reflected in the writings of the recent popes. Pius X, rightly considered the architect of the present reform, defined the role of music for all time:

> Sacred music, as an integral part of the solemn liturgy, shares in its general purpose, which is the glory of God and the sanctification and edification of the faithful. It contributes to the increase of decorum and splendor of ecclesiastical ceremonies, and since its principal function is to adorn with suitable melody the liturgical text, . . . its proper purpose is to add greater efficacy to the text itself, so that by this means the faithful may be more easily moved to devotion and disposed to receive in themselves the fruits of grace proper to the celebration of the sacred mysteries (*Motu Proprio*, No. 1).

Pius XII expressed the "keen desire of the Church that

all of the faithful sing their hymns and chant their song of praise and thanksgiving to him who is King of Kings and Source of every blessing" (*Mediator Dei,* No. 83). In his encyclical letter of December, 1955, this same Shepherd restated the truth that "the freedom of the artist" is "in no way restricted or destroyed, but actually ennobled and perfected, when it is made subject to the divine law" (No. 26). This is true when it is made subject to the law of the Church in establishing liturgical norms, whereby it is given the negative function of preventing anything that "might distract the faithful" from "entering into sacred music, which is the servant, as it were, of the sacred liturgy" (*Musicae Sacrae Disciplina,* No. 30).

The 1958 Instruction further unites the concepts of congregational singing and the singing of the choir by noting that "of its nature the Mass demands that all those who are present should participate, each in his own proper way" (No. 22). All of the papal directives of the past sixty years have essayed to enhance the role of the choir while trying to restore the role of the faithful to its proper place. Some degree of participation was achieved throughout the Catholic world, but the barrier of the Latin language proved too difficult to overcome. It was to the Second Vatican Council that there fell the happy task of restoring the earlier tradition of Mass in the vernacular, and thereby allowing the restoration of music to come into its own. The directives since 1903 remain in effect, save that the English language may be allowed; the promotion of the English language demands reinterpretation of former decrees, and the formation of a new, and authentic, tradition. The guiding principles for this tradition are within the Constitution.

The Role of Music According to the Constitution

> Pastors of souls must realize that, when the liturgy is cele-
> brated, something more is required than the mere observa-
> tion of the laws governing valid and licit celebration; it is
> their duty also to ensure that the faithful take part fully
> aware of what they are doing, actively engaged in the rite,
> and enriched by its effects (Constitution, Art. 11).

> In the restoration and promotion of the sacred liturgy,
> this full and active participation by all the people is the
> aim to be considered before all else (Art. 21).

> Servers, lectors, commentators and members of the choir
> . . . exercise a genuine liturgical function. They ought,
> therefore, to discharge their office with a sincere piety and
> decorum demanded by so exalted a ministry and rightly
> expected of them by God's people (Art. 29).

The first aim is the full participation by all the faithful,
with no denial to the role of the choir, but an actual en-
hancement, for this document clearly refers to the work
of the members of choir as the discharge of an "office." The
tradition encouraging full participation by people and choir,
evident in past ages, and prominent in the legislation of
recent decades, is the norm for future greatness, a greatness
foreseen by the Constitution on the Sacred Liturgy.

Communal. Worship is the expression of faith; as such it
is the worship of the faithful, of all who believe in Christ
as present "to his Church, especially in her liturgical celebrations . . . in the sacrifice of the Mass . . . in the person
of his minister . . . under the eucharistic species . . . in the
sacraments" (Constitution, Art. 7). It is the worship of the
entire community of believers, not just the domain of a part
of that community. The long history of silent spectators at

Mass is coming to an end. The "Low Mass" is no longer to be a ceremony performed by one, and witnessed by many; the "High Mass" will no longer be viewed as the combined singing of priest and choir for the benefit of the congregation. All have an important part in that worship.

It might be well to note, however, that the people are also to listen, and that this is a form of prayer. As long as the principle of their rightful role is safeguarded, special circumstances would see the choir performing a portion reserved to the people, but never as a matter of practice. More pertinent to the value of listening, however, is the performance of the choir's role, which will allow for contemplation, just as the singing of the Gospel by the priest or deacon enables everyone to receive the Word of God into his heart.

Hierarchic. Although the community worships together, it is called together only by God, and so is hierarchic in nature; its prayer depends upon the constituted hierarchy, and is ordered in its structure by a division of functions. The confusion of roles led to the sad state of the separation of music from the liturgy. It is interesting to note that the choir and priest are seen by the Council fathers to enjoy a "ministry," and that both are to serve the needs of the people. Music is to share with the liturgy the nature of being hierarchic, by allowing each to perform his, and only his, role as a matter of principle.

Pastoral. The prominent mark of the Council is its pastoral concern, its involvement over the needs of the ordinary parish. When both art and liturgical thought are rooted in the life of the people, and spring up in forms of devotion that are "popular" without being "vulgar," then Church music will have reached its goal. A music that is alien to the people is as alien to the true notion of liturgical music as one that is estranged from the spirit of the liturgy, and purely external to its workings. Music is pastoral when it enables all to grow in an understanding of the sacred rites that are "within the people's powers of comprehension" (Art. 34).

Didactic. If the liturgy nourishes the faithful, it also instructs them; it is not only *mater*, but *magistra*. "In the liturgy, God speaks to his people, and Christ is still proclaiming his Gospel. And the people reply to God both by song and prayer" (Art. 34). The music of the liturgy enjoys this same teaching function; it takes the sacred texts and clothes them with newer shades of meaning, makes them more capable of eliciting a response. It is not only instructive, but formative; not only attracts the mind, but captures the soul; it explains the faith, but more importantly still, it stirs the faithful.

Furthermore, music is capable of instructing the people in what the liturgy is; a learning by doing is intended here, which means that the music will have to appeal to modern man, invite him to take part, and move him to take part well.

The Great Rediscovery of Music

The above characteristics of the liturgy, applicable to the music of the liturgy as well, enlarge our understanding of the importance of the musician in liturgical restoration. The vision of music as a utilitarian art, determined by considerations of the practical, is the beginning of the "Great Rediscovery" of music, a time of creativity that will wed words with music once again, and possibly rival the period of the Gregorian chant in excellence.

The desire for liturgical awareness and musical reform has joined both fields of study together. Both movements may be considered as part of one activity, each portion colored by respect for the other. Both are joined in a negative way by their concern for the problems that the use of the vernacular languages will entail; the liturgist must see to it that the rites are clearly outlined, well ordered, and make use of good, if not outstanding, translations and texts; the musician must be at pains to make his art a working art as well as one of beauty, and to enhance the Mass with further majesty.

The Principles Governing Church Music

From the nature of liturgical music, the first and foremost principle is that enunciated by Pius XII: "the chants and sacred music which are immediately joined with the Church's liturgical worship should be conducive to the lofty end for which they are intended" (*Musicae Sacrae Disciplina*, No. 41). In other words, music must be true to itself, and to its purpose, and so possess those qualities which Pius X laid down as being traditional. There are three such qualities.

Holiness. This stems directly from the closeness of the sacred music to the liturgy, which is the worship of the thrice-holy God by the people whom he means to make holy. Sacred music must not be marked by a similarity to the profane, but possess a quality of "otherness," without being foreign to modern man. It is to be simple and restrained, reverent and wholly intent upon its fixed purpose of praise. Above all, it is to be remembered that music "makes holy" the listener and the singer, sharing, as we have seen, in the general purpose of the liturgy—the sanctification of men.

Goodness of form. Church music must be true art, composed and performed with skill, and sung by a people whose main concern is the mastery of a sturdy Christian life informed by the worship of the Church.

Universality. It will not be feasible, except at large gatherings where many nations and languages are represented, to expect a universality of form whereby one composition could serve many translations. (The Constitution does allow for the retention of the ancient Latin for such gatherings, but this is an exception, and not the rule.) A universality of expression, however, is not only possible, but mandatory. By this is meant that the various languages, into which the Mass is being translated, are to be intimately bound up with the music used to express the sacred texts. The chant could be universal, because the language intimately joined to it was universal; now that is no longer true. To model the music of the liturgy of the Church upon the chant, which does possess the above three characteristics, means only that music is to do for the many languages what the chant accomplished for the Latin (and at an age when such a musical idiom was a part of the culture of the people).

The latter truth reveals the task of the Church musician today.

CHAPTER TWO

WHO SINGS IN CHURCH?

At any time prior to the Constitution on the Sacred Liturgy, the replies to this simple question would be as varied as answers relating to queries on personal tastes in music, or the practices of individual parishes throughout the country. The question is not phrased in terms of current practice, however, but is hopefully worded with an eye to the future. It should then receive the response of the Fathers of the Council to the question, "Who is to sing in Church?"; and this reply is "Everyone!" It is their declaration that

> liturgical services pertain to the whole body of the Church; they manifest it and have effects upon it, but they concern the individual members of the Church in different ways, according to their differing rank, office, or actual participation (Constitution, Art. 26).

The whole body (everyone) is to sing; this is clear from the conciliar decree. It is equally clear, however, that everyone is not to sing everything! This truth flows from the very nature of the parish as a community which mirrors, and shares in, the perfect community of the Church Catholic. Every true community is a well-ordered unity, dependent upon the concerted efforts of each component. For the ordinary parish to function as a community at worship, it must first be convinced that it *is* a community, and this is done when each element respects the role of the other.

The parish must next be convinced that it is a praying community, one actively engaged in the worshipful action of Christ. This is an area immediately involving the work of the priest, following the directives established by the bishop of the diocese. It must be borne in mind that personal prayer and public prayer do not exclude each other, but the former should be formed by the latter, and both are included within the format of liturgical worship.

Lastly, the Christian community is a singing community, for it is a properly Catholic attitude to recognize that music in the liturgy is sung prayer, intrinsic to the liturgy.

Unless one understands the community and identifies himself with it, he cannot serve it, and without such service the very notion of community is weakened. Should this service be withheld, all attempts to revitalize the liturgy are doomed, for a sense of community is central to the development of a good, workable, and beautiful liturgy. It is a problem to be faced squarely by people, priest and choir.

The Role of the Priest-President

The fact that the priest will no longer have to "read" the various parts of the Mass belonging to choir and people, as was formerly the case, in no way destroys his role of prime importance to the celebration of the Mass. His noble and exalted position is actually enhanced and put into greater relief. He will stand out as the president of the community that he truly is. He prays in the name of all present, and alone prays the great prayer of the Canon-Action; he is the minister of the Word and dispenser of the Sacrament to his people. All of these functions are discussed at further length in the *Priest's Guide to Parish Worship,* a part of the Parish Worship Program.

For our purposes we can note that the priest oversees the program of participation in his parish, directs its achievements, guides those who enjoy a specialized province of activity, and constantly supports and encourages the entire work. His support (and praise, which can work miracles in welding the members of a choir into a workable whole) is only secondary to his primary function as leader of prayer, whether that prayer is sung or merely recited. Of a truth, the people and choir do not sing *at* Mass—they sing *the* Mass.

His singing sets the tone of the entire service of worship. The Latin portions should be sung in as perfect and flawless a style as possible. The English portions demand a different treatment; these include the lessons from Scripture, the greetings, and the invitations (opening lines) to such prayers as the Gloria and Creed. The following suggestions may prove useful.

1. Good recitation (or "monotoning") is dependent upon good reading, and demands a thorough familiarity with the text, for the proclamation of the lessons is really a public reading.

2. Unlike Latin, each English syllable should not be equal in length to every other syllable, although the final effect to be attained is smoothness. In singing, the principal vowel sound must necessarily be prolonged somewhat, and auxiliary vowels clearly differentiated, since this is the way we speak; consonants must be carefully articulated, yet, if exaggerated, they endanger the flow and continuity of the

sung line. Consonants are not musical sounds, and so should be actually passed over quickly.

3. The pitch must be perfectly kept to the note on which the sentences are sung, and this demands care at the beginning and end of sentences.

4. The greetings of the priest should be precisely that; they should encourage a response at least equal in enthusiasm and vigor. The opening words of the Gloria and Creed, for example, should also invite a response—the response of the entire prayer which he begins.

From the role of the priest at worship, we see clearly that he stands in direct relationship to the people; he addresses them, and begins their prayer; his Preface precedes their song of "Holy, holy, holy," and his blessing upon them moves them to assent to all that has happened with their final "Amen." With the people, he listens to the Word of God read by the lectors, and contemplates the texts sung by the choir. With the people and choir, he continues the Gloria and Creed, thereby encouraging the entire congregation. The Constitution proclaims that each person should perform *only* his role (Art. 28) but this need not be held to too rigidly; this article is intended to do away with useless duplication, such as the quiet recitation of the Agnus Dei while the congregation sings this prayer. Communal participation does imply that priest and people may sing (or say) the Ordinary of the Mass together.

The Role of the People

To promote active participation, the people should be encouraged to take part by means of acclamations, responses, psalmody, antiphons, and songs, as well as by actions, gestures, and bodily attitudes. And at the proper times all should observe a reverent silence (Constitution, Art. 30).

There are parts of the Mass that pertain to the people as their proper sharing in the Mass; no one would dispute that this has been traditionally held, at least in theory. Such parts include the responses to the prayers and greetings of the celebrant. The brief acclamations, such as Kyrie and Agnus Dei pose no real problem. Their simple, strong character as popular invocations demand that they be treated without any attempt at elaboration. The Sanctus hymn, as the foremost "hymn" of the Mass, belongs to priest and people together, as is evident from the usual wording of the Preface. The Creed by its placement at the conclusion of the Service of the Word should not be an elaborate composition; its length would seem to indicate that it may be alternated by choir and people. The same might also be done for the Gloria, and although it is a part proper to the people, there is nothing to prevent the choir from singing it with the people, or even entirely by themselves. As long as the functions proper to choir and people are mutually respected, and there is no danger of clinging to past methods of performance which left the people silent, the choir can sing a well-written and impressive Gloria on certain occasions.

The article quoted above, however, also mentions "psalmody, antiphons, and songs," and this leads to a further interpretation of the role of the people in the Mass, without in the least suppressing the privileged role of the choir. The chants of the Mass where psalmody (and antiphons) are employed fall into two categories—processional chants and songs of response.

The latter type would refer to the Gradual; it is the response to God's Word from hearts that have received that Word. The 'processional chants' describes those antiphons that accompanied the psalm verses during the three times when processions occurred: the Introit accompanied the procession of the sacred ministers into the sanctuary; the Offertory and Communion chants were used while the people moved to the altar to give, and receive, the sacred gifts. Traditionally, these portions of the Mass have been the role of the choir, and the antiphons themselves have received the fullest musical treatment, with the psalm verses being sung to simpler settings.

The people are encouraged to take part, and to join with the choir, when possible, in singing these chants. What may be done? A certain flexibility seems to provide the answer, together with the creation of a new and authentic tradition. Since there is no clear reason to forbid the choir from ever singing the Gloria entirely, and very serious reason to suggest that people and choir alternate in the singing of such hymns as the Gloria and Creed, the further possibility exists that the people might be given a role in the singing of certain portions of the Proper. The division into Ordinary and Proper parts rests upon the impossibility of the parish to prepare the movable chants for each Sunday. What has been proposed, therefore, is that the chants be so arranged as to allow the people to join with the choir.

The Gradual might be sung by people and choir if it is a short, simple melody. They might more easily sing a simple Alleluia, or short responsorial phrase, to the verses of the choir's text.

For the processional chants, it must be remembered that their value lies in the fact that they are intended to cover the entire period of the entrance procession, Offertory and Communion rites, and the antiphons and psalms should be so arranged to allow for additional verses to be sung when the need arises. If the antiphon is itself a short, simple refrain, the people and choir might sing it together, with the choir singing the verses, although the simpler settings of the verses would certainly not prove difficult for the congregation if the words were available to them.

With people and choir working together to sing the Mass, the people always taking the simpler parts, and the choir responsible for the more highly developed forms, there comes into being the real distribution of roles demanded by the liturgy. The choir is the leader of the entire body of the faithful, and their support; the people follow their lead, listen to the choir at the proper times, and are moved to greater devotion by the richness of the choral music and by the spirit of participation that such a communal celebration imparts.

The Role of the Choir

From the Constitution on the Sacred Liturgy, an important principle emerges, namely the determination of a genuine liturgical ministry by reason of the function performed, rather than by some juridical appointment. Not only does the entire body of the faithful enjoy a genuine liturgical function, but certain members of the laity as well, such as commentators and members of the choir (which would include women singers). The specialized ministry of the choir is given considerable emphasis by the Council fathers, despite the prominence now accorded to the role that the congregation must play.

The principal role of the choir is as a part of the body of

the faithful, a role shared by all, lectors as well as choir members, priest as well as parishioner; all are joined as one body to Christ the Lord, and offer his perfect sacrifice to the Father through the agency of his priesthood. Such an attitude must needs prevail; it is the problem of realizing that we *are* a community, and that Mass is a communal action, in which all contribute to the building up of the faith which we profess by sacred rites.

The role of leading the people and supporting the singing of the congregation is of importance, especially when one considers the practice of past and silent centuries. The people need the support of the choir for the responses and Ordinary of the Mass; should the choir *not* sing these people's parts, then they may be poorly sung. One might consider the relationship of the choir to the people in the light of the use of the organ in sustaining the choir; as the organ should not overpower the sound of the choir, but gently and firmly support their voices, so should the choir encourage the people. It is needless to point out that the congregation will never possess the skills of a trained choir, and depends upon the choir for its own singing. This educative sphere of the choir's activity is again based upon the inter-dependence of the distinguished roles within the liturgy, and in no way violates the principle of each role singing *only* its part, for the principal parts of the choir are those which lead the people.

The Choir's Proper Sphere

In suggesting that choir and people co-operate in singing certain portions of the Ordinary, and Proper (Introit, Offertory, Communion), by alternating with one another on occasion, the direction of the Constitution is respected. Alternation seems to be a solution, and as such it is proposed primarily to the composers, and ultimately to choirmasters. The role of the choir, in the light of conciliar directives and recent pronouncements, is never to minimize or negate the active participation of all who are present for Mass. The role of encouraging the people is not merely a temporary service, but a constant endeavor; if the choir leads, and the people sing with them by alternating phrases or verses, then these roles (and not the facile division of Proper and Ordinary) will determine the liturgy of present and revised rites, and a true Catholic sense of community will be created.

The fusion of the ideas of "leadership of the people" and "performance of proper function" which lies open to musicians allows for polyphonic and modern music to be employed to the fullest degree possible. The flexibility already mentioned, and it is considerable, insures what must be insisted upon: at all Masses that are not "private" in nature (priest and server, or sparse congregation) there is always a role for the choir. At sung Mass (High Mass) the supplementary hymns, such as at the Offertory or Communion, as well as processional and recessional anthems belong to the choir if they are to be festive and true celebrations. Only the rich harmony of experienced voices can add a note of majesty and power, and move even the poorest of singers among the people to a greater love of God. (There is no need to mention sacred concerts, nor the roles supplied by choirs at other functions in addition to the Mass, for the provisions of the choir within the eucharistic sacrifice already distinguish this noble "office.")

The fulfillment of the role of the choir is necessary, or the liturgy will be in a sadder state than in times past, and we shall be saddled by tired and unimaginative recitatives. Thus, although the singing of the Proper by the choir, and the Ordinary by the people may be the division of roles within a given parish, the attitude of the Council and common sense in dealing with matters liturgical enjoins the distinction of roles to rest upon leadership. The enrichment of settings, whereby the people may even have a role in difficult passages (a *cantus firmus*, for example), can only be the activity of the choir; but then, the entire work of the liturgy is dependent upon the choir, and membership in the choir is truly a vocation, and a call to responsibility.

CHAPTER THREE

THE MUSIC OF THE MASS

"The treasury of sacred music is to be preserved and fostered with great care" (Constitution, Art. 113). This is the heritage drawn from the musicians within the Church, and the present decrees do not intend to jettison the work of centuries for music that will not last; it is also the heritage of the past, and the Constitution does not wish the congregation's song to be cast aside for the sake of a musical elite. There does exist the real need to make adaptations of the chant and other forms of music, and the task will prove an arduous one. At the same time, there is the necessity of creating new music, and such creative activity is the essence of the matter of providing a rich inheritance of musical tradition for the future ages, in which the revised liturgy shall be thoroughly familiar and relevant. The shape of things to come presents both a challenge and an appeal to the musicians.

In pointing out the need for adapting and creating the music of the liturgy, the guiding norm will always be the necessity of *true art* as the only useful vehicle for expressing the meaning of the sacred texts. There are many different musical styles that present themselves to the consideration of the artist, including such authentic expressions of liturgical texts as closely approximate the vitality of the Negro spirituals; such forms should not be accepted unless they prove their artistic merit, but they should not be condemned without a hearing. While making use of a number of chant-hymns and mono-syllabic chants that can be adapted to the English language (because of its strong and varying accents), the musician is asked to look forward to the day when we will have a truly authentic art growing out of the new English liturgy.

What Must Be Done

In principle, the English language must be maintained throughout the entire program of participation; as has been noted already, this will allow for unity of direction and continuity of practice. It will help to make the people "at home" with the sung rites once they have come to appreciate the English Low Mass. Such a coherent pattern of worship will cut through the initial bewilderment (and even resentment) that will come with the changes. If the revised liturgy is to become the life-giving reality that it is by nature, then such a singleness of approach is demanded.

In practice, during this period of transition, the Latin will remain as an alternate, and unless some further development takes place, it is quite possible that the High Mass will make use of the Ordinary chants in English, and the Proper in Latin, or vice-versa. This is certainly one way in which the musical heritage of the past can be preserved. It must be remembered that the present time will see a variety of possible solutions, but that these are only makeshifts until the High Mass will be entirely in English. It is proposed that choir-directors make full use of whatever good English music is available, and do all that lies within their power to bring about a meaningful program, in which the choir and the congregation are acquainted with the very best in English hymns and chants. Fortunately, we are gifted with a good number of talented musicians in this country who are aware of the true bounds of liturgical music, and the need for introducing the vernacular music as soon as possible. Although the use of English is lawful, it is not obligatory in the sung Mass at this time; the retention of Latin without any attempt to introduce the vernacular is a violation of the spirit of the liturgy as envisioned by the Council. This is an age of transition, but it can also be an age similar to the centuries that saw the development of the Gregorian Chant, and which gave the Church a hegemony in the field of music that has influenced all subsequent growth.

Music at the Sung Rites

At present, there is a problem of repertoire; we will have to wait until a good selection of approved music is at hand, and since sung ceremonies are to be preferred to any other type of celebration (especially on Sundays and feasts) the musician is faced with the problem of what to do in the interim. The easiest solution might possibly be found in the principle of flexibility and experimentation, and in the relaxation of an unnecessary rigidity in distinguishing between the "Low" and the "High" Mass.

The High Mass is that form of celebration in which *every* participant, by reason of his liturgical office, sings those parts which the tradition of the Church has joined to musical forms. This means not only the portions sung by the choir and the people, but the specifically *priestly* segments as well, which actually determine whether or not the Mass is a "High" Mass. This being so, only those Masses are technically High Masses in which the people sing their responses to the sung greetings of celebrant or deacon, conclude the priest's orations with their sung "Amen," and continue the singing of such prayers as the Gloria and Creed that have been intoned by the president of the assembly. Keeping this distinction in mind, two suggestions for experimentation can be adduced.

1. The introduction of English portions into the existing High Mass structure can be done gradually. Beginning with the Lord Have Mercy in place of the Kyrie, the Ordinary parts can be replaced by the vernacular versions in the space of a relatively short time.

2. Without discontinuing the sung Mass, it has been proposed that the celebrant *not* sing his parts, or, in other words, that the ceremony not be a High Mass technically speaking. The people and choir would still sing their parts, however, although much time and care will have to be spent before they will be able to sing all of the Proper and Ordinary. This proposal considers the fact that, since it is not a High Mass in the true sense of the word, the choir will be enabled to experiment with *good* forms of adaptation and new music. Poor music should never be introduced, under any pretext; it is an unprofitable servant! Musical settings can be had even at present, with some slight modifications, and may also be found in the music books of the non-Catholic denominations, for the Protestant communions have had a long history of good music for both choir and people, and these may be borrowed with profit.

For example, the new *Service Book and Hymnal* of the

Lutheran Church in America contains many superb pieces of music that will fit the approved, official translation. The arrangement of the Kyrie by Harold W. Gilbert is a beautiful and powerful refrain, and the Old Scottish Chant for the Gloria could readily be adapted to the version which Catholic worship in this country will employ. The famous "1940 Hymnal" of the Episcopalian Church contains several settings for the Communion Service, of which the arrangements for the Sanctus hymn are worthy and welcome selections for our purposes. Then, too, there is the work of Catholic composers who are skillfully and tastefully seeking to provide new music.

It is hoped that the "Low Mass" and the "High Mass" will not be categories denoting exclusive use or absence of music, but that the flexibility already evident in many parishes will be allowed to continue, and that every Mass will be an occasion of joyful song and prayer.

The Music Program and the Low Mass

The development of the Low Mass program has seen the rise of rites that are certainly more solemn than those celebrations in which no singing takes place, and more truly celebrations as far as the people are concerned than High Masses sung by the celebrant and only one other person, usually the organist.

The proposal that the Ordinary and Proper chants in English be introduced at what is technically *not* a High Mass, will also serve the purposes of the Low Mass with hymns as well. As such, it will be a Low Mass with experimental music, and would be one way to try out musical settings without the solemnity of the High Mass structure.

The format would be that of the program for Low Mass now in use throughout various parts of the country. The regimen of participation follows the principle that hymns and/or psalms should parallel the Proper chants of the High Mass; furthermore, the music selected should be appropriate to their position during the Mass, or reflect the liturgical attitudes proper to the various feasts and seasons of the liturgical year. In brief, the Low Mass with hymns should *always* be patterned after the High Mass.

This program has placed hymns and/or psalms in those periods of the Mass which are covered by the processional chants, and a brief refrain as a song of meditation after the Scripture lesson. If no hymn is used at one of these positions, the verses of the Proper might possibly be recited, and when the hymn is used, it would take the place of the corresponding Proper part as far as the music is concerned.

At such Masses the role of the choir is again one of importance. The hesitancy and possible inability of the congregation can be overcome by the strength and eagerness of the choir; in some cases leaders of the congregation have worked to catch the "mood" of the people, but a lack of proper support only made a failure where a success would otherwise have been inevitable. The use of the choir facilitates the singing of hymns at Low Mass; the choir can alternate with the people in singing short antiphons to the psalm verses, and they can certainly add extra solemnity to any program of Low Mass with hymns that demand trained voices and experience for their proper execution.

What Hymns to Choose

The use of hymns *at* Mass should match the use of the texts *of* the Mass, capture their mood and spirit, and conform to the standards set for liturgical music. The songs of meditation between the readings, if these can properly be called "songs," should be short refrains of a reflective nature; the Alleluia which is oftentimes repeated as a refrain, should be a simple melody, unlike the long melismatic chants developed by the chanters of the Middle Ages.

When a song is used to parallel the processional chants, it should be chosen because of its appropriateness to the very idea of the chant it parallels. This is the first principle of selectivity, and should be employed whenever possible. The various parallel chants are identifiable with key notions, which ideas serve as a guide in choosing material.

Introit. The Introit antiphon and psalm is a processional song to accompany the entrance of the sacred ministers (celebrant and servers, at the Low Mass), and it covers what would otherwise be a lengthy period of silence. Psalm 42, so long identified with the concept of drawing near to the altar, would be of considerable value as an entrance hymn for a Low Mass program. Also the hymns *Praise to the Lord, On this day the first of days*, and *O Holy Lord, by all adored*.

Kyrie. This is a short invocation to Christ the Lord, simple and strong in its approach, masterfully terse in its phrasing. It should not be treated elaborately. In Low Masses this could best be recited, or sung to a simple setting (such as the Alleluia refrain appended to the hymn *The strife is o'er*, by Palestrina)—but never replaced by a hymn as such.

Gloria. Although this is a simple chant, it is certainly susceptible of musical embellishment. It might be stated here that normally the Introit, Gradual, Offertory and Communion songs, together with a hymn of thanksgiving (recessional) are replaced by hymns for the Low Mass program.

Gradual and other intervening chants. These chants do not accompany a procession, nor fill in an empty period of the Mass. They have instead an autonomous position, and are reflective prayer. The history of their usage—psalm verses sung by the cantor or schola, with a congregational verse or refrain—suggests their special function. A brief refrain, such as an antiphon to a Gelineau Psalm, would serve the function of this meditative song of response. A three-fold Alleluia would also be practical here.

Creed. At a Low Mass in which there is a Creed, it is best recited. This would certainly clarify its character as a formula of faith also used during the celebration of other sacraments, such as Baptism and Confirmation.

Offertory (antiphon and psalm). These songs are rarely used to signify a preparation of gifts, although that is the action which they actually embellish, but have a more direct relationship to the sacrifice for which they provide both the meaning and the motive. Any psalm suitable to the season would be appropriate here, as would the hymns: *Father, see thy children; What thou gavest*; and *O Knight of might and splendor.*

Sanctus. This short text is the central chant of the Mass; it has a priority not only of place, but of role as well. It belongs to the priest and the people together, and should be in the nature of an acclamation.

Agnus Dei. Of considerably less importance than either the Sanctus, or the Kyrie which it closely resembles, the Agnus Dei should be understood and recited as an acclamation or royal greeting addressed to Christ.

Communion (antiphon and psalm). This is the processional song of the Eucharistic banquet, and parallels the Introit and the Offertory antiphons. That song is needed during this portion of the Mystery of the Mass cannot be denied; it helps to build up the sense of community, makes the people aware of the parish altar as the Table of the Lord, and provides fitting meditation for the communicants. Psalms 22, 33, and 147 recommend themselves for use at this part of the Mass, as does the Great Hallel Psalm 135, whose antiphon connotes the love and mercy that God has given to those whom he has ransomed. A suitable hymn might be *Lord who at thy first Eucharist didst pray;* others would be *Draw nigh and take the Body of the Lord, Let all mortal flesh keep silence,* and *O Lord, with wondrous mystery.*

It might be well to add that the psalms need not always be selected because of liturgical appropriateness. The example of the Roman Missal can be adduced to show that the psalms at the Offertory and Communion are rarely related to the action. They are more in the nature of "general hymns." In ancient times, the psalms were taken numerically, and it would be well to select the psalm that is used during the Mass itself, if that is possible. The use of general hymns should not be discouraged, but the principle of choosing hymns that suitably accompany an action of the Mass should be used as the normal method of procedure.

The recessional hymn should be proper to the feast or season, or be a hymn of praise and thanksgiving: *God Father, praise and glory; Father, we thank thee; Praise to the holiest; Praise the Lord of heaven; Holy God we praise thy name.*

When hymns are chosen in accordance with the Church Year, the text of the Gospel might be taken into consideration. On the fourth Sunday after Epiphany, for example, the Gospel depicts Christ calming the storm; a fitting hymn would be *God moves in a mysterious way*. For the four hymns used at Low Mass, the following gives an indication of hymns that reflect the meaning of the appropriate season.

Introit: Jesus Christ is ris'n today; Singers, sing, and trumpets play; All glory, laud and honor; Virgin-born we bow before thee.

Offertory: As with gladness men of old (Epiphany); Heart of Christ; Hymn for the poor souls; Psalm 46 (Ascension).

Communion: O Come, all ye faithful; A great and mighty wonder; The royal banners forward go; At the Lamb's high feast we sing.

Recessional: The strife is o'er (not referring to any mistakes in singing among people or choir-masters that might have happened during Mass!); Hail the day that sees him rise; Songs of thankfulness and praise.

Lastly, the hymns appropriate to the occasion for which the Mass is being celebrated should be taken into account when choosing the music. In particular, weddings and funerals will make use of hymns that are appropriate; Psalm 127 for the former, and 129 for the latter. It cannot be insisted upon sufficiently that these occasions should have a communal nature, and this should provide an opportunity for a good hymn to be of service.

In any event, whether the Mass be one in honor of a certain saint, in celebration of one of the mysteries of our redemption (feast day or period of the liturgical year), or special to one occasion or another, the hymns must be chosen for their ability to fit into the framework of the Mass, and should never be based upon personal likes and dislikes alone. The selection of hymns must never be left to mere arbitrary choice without consideration for the nature of the Eucharistic Sacrifice or for the sanctification of time by means of the Mass.

CHAPTER FOUR

MUSIC AT OTHER FUNCTIONS

Popular devotions of the Christian people are to be highly commended, provided they accord with the laws and norms of the Church, above all when they are ordered by the Apostolic See.

Devotions proper to the individual Churches also have special dignity if they are undertaken by mandate of the bishops according to customs or books lawfully approved.

But these devotions should be so drawn up that they harmonize with the liturgical seasons, accord with the liturgy, are in some fashion derived from it, and lead the people to it, since, in fact, the liturgy by its very nature surpasses any of them (Constitution, Art. 13).

This statement by the pope and the other bishops of the Church follows closely upon their declaration of belief that the liturgy is "the summit toward which the activity of the Church is directed," and "the fount from which all her power flows" (Art. 10). Since large numbers of the faithful have drawn strength from the devotions that have grown up within the Church, the Council fathers have wisely upheld the value that such *pia exercitia* have, and wish them to be placed within the perspective of the liturgical life of the Church. Although the content of these services often leaves much to be desired, the mere fact that they employ vernacular prayers and hymns guarantees them an important help in educating the people to the new changes in our forms of worship.

The liturgical hour of Vespers has its origin in a popular devotion, and perhaps the devotions of our day will determine the very shape of the liturgy in future years. For the present, these services perform an invaluable service to the Church; these devotions increase devotion; these popular rites can lead us to an understanding of the Mass rites as being truly "popular." If they are patterned after the prayer of the liturgy, and direct our hearts to God our Father through his Son, they will fill out the devotional life of the Christian, and make his share of the liturgical actions of Christ more meaningful.

The Bible Service

> Bible services should be encouraged, especially on the vigils of the more solemn feasts, on some weekdays in Advent and Lent, and on Sundays and feast days. . . . a deacon or some other person authorized by the bishop should preside over the celebration (Constitution, Art. 35).

Among the popular services to be encouraged is the so-called Bible Devotion, or "Vigil," which is termed a *celebration*, since it is parallel to the Fore-Mass, or Celebration of the Word. They have been treated in a separate booklet of the Parish Worship Program entitled *The Bible Service*. Their development is rather recent, but they present a larger framework for instruction in the faith than the novena services, and are readily adaptable to any occasion. When the Bible Service takes place as a Church service, as distinct from classroom or home usage, two types of music are employed. First, there are the hymns that open and close the service, and these should serve to introduce the theme, and complete its development; secondly, there are the meditative songs (usually psalms) that follow each reading of Scripture. The service itself consists of several Scripture readings that deal with one theme; each reading is followed by a sung response and a prayer, while the homily or homilies of the celebrant tie the readings together into a coherent unity. An action, or sacred rite, brings the entire service to a conclusion.

These devotions can fit most any occasion. For example, a Bible Service on ashes, tracing their usage throughout the Old Testament, could precede the "action" of the blessing and distribution of this sacramental at the start of Lent. Any blessing can be preceded by such celebrations of the Word that make the rite clearer, and the "action" reveals the meaning of the Word of God all the more fittingly. Since a deep unity exists between the Scripture readings and the concluding rite, this same unity must guide the choice of hymns. A fitting Entrance Hymn for a Bible Service on Ash Wednesday would be "Lord, Who Throughout These Forty Days"; for a scriptural devotion in honor of Christ the King, the opening hymn might be "Crown Him with Many Crowns." This same principle of unified treatment should guide the choice of the closing hymn as well, with the understanding that a hymn of praise and thanksgiving is always a fitting Recessional.

A second principle might guide the choice of the opening hymn, namely that any opening hymn may fit the nature of the ceremony. In this case, a Psalm or hymn to the Word of God would be an apt choice. Psalm 94 offers itself as the ideal scriptural song, especially since the Bible Service resembles Matins with its readings and psalms. Unfortunately, there are few hymns that deal with the Scriptures with which Catholics are familiar, although many good ones exist in non-Catholic service-books.

The meditative songs merit a different treatment. These parallel the Gradual chants of the Mass, and are the people's response to the readings from the Bible. They should provide an opportunity for God's people to "sort out the Scriptures" and be nourished by them, and so should continue the theme of the readings. They should not distract the congregation from meditating upon the mystery that is being presented to them through the readings, homilies and prayers.

Although hymns might serve the purpose, especially as they are familiar to the people, the ideal songs of response are the Psalms. The venerable tradition of the Church holds that merely human words are inadequate to serve as our response to God's Word; since that same Word is its own response, the Church has seen fit to make of the psalms her meditation upon what God has spoken. Psalms that refer to the topic of the readings should be used, but it might prove easier to use only one psalm, with the verses divided so that the entire psalm would cover the several lessons. For example, a Bible Service concerning Mary's role as the "Ark of the Covenant" would make use of the *Magnificat*; a few verses after each of the three readings would complete the singing of this canticle.

Since hymns are not forbidden as meditative chants, it is perhaps better to use only one hymn, with a different verse after each reading. This simplifies the devotion, and prevents confusion. When hymns are being chosen, however, whether as processional songs or songs of meditation, their future use by the congregation at Mass might be taken into account. The Bible Service is an excellent "parish rehearsal" for the Sunday Mass, and assures the choir that at least some of the people will know the hymn, making their leadership even more effective.

Benediction of the Most Blessed Sacrament

The Constitution itself presents us with the principles of music selection, in the quotation introducing this chapter. The hymns, like the devotions they enhance, should "harmonize with the liturgical seasons, accord with the liturgy," be "derived from it, and lead the people to it." They should reflect the pattern of liturgical prayer, echo the mystery of the Church year now being proclaimed, and increase our desire to do the Eucharist once again. This is especially to be hoped for in the choice of hymns for Benediction. All too often the same hymns are sung, and consequently sung poorly; a choice of hymns from the repertoire learned in the low Mass program would do much to make this liturgical function impressive and meaningful.

The development of Benediction arose with the Marian devotions prominent in Italy and France during the Middle Ages, and the use of a Marian hymn is a beautiful custom that should be retained. "Virgin-born, We Bow Before Thee" is entirely in keeping with this tradition, and with the adoration of Christ as well.

Since the Eucharist is a "banquet in which Christ is eaten, the mind is filled with grace, and a pledge of future glory given us" (Constitution, Art. 47), hymns which treat of these themes would be most welcome. An Easter hymn would be an appropriate opening hymn, such as "At the Lamb's High Feast We Sing," for the paschal significance of the Eucharist is too often neglected, and the sacrifice of Christ is a "paschal banquet." The notion of the Eucharist as our food would be fitting as well, for it would "lead to the liturgy" by encouraging the reception of Holy Communion; one of the purposes of Benediction is to increase our desire to be one with Christ, and to receive him under forms of bread and wine. A suitable closing hymn would depict the joys of heaven, or the Church Triumphant, centering upon the "pledge of future glory" that is contained within the Sacrament of the Altar.

In general, the selection of hymns for use at Benediction must be in accord with the one hymn that the Church demands we sing, namely the *Tantum Ergo* (which now may be sung in English), the concluding verses to the *Pange Lingua* of Thomas Aquinas.

The Forty Hours

The Forty Hours' Devotion, as well as the procession on the feast of Corpus Christi, have noticeably declined in popularity over the past years, and one reason for this may have been the unintelligibility of the rites. The lengthy litany, with its versicles and prayers, are now to be sung in English, and several translations with musical accompaniment have been available for some time (cf. bibliography). The processions in honor of the Blessed Sacrament provide a good opportunity for the hymns suggested for use at Benediction, especially the longer ones from the office of Corpus Christi.

The chanting of the Litany of the Saints emphasizes the

role of the choir as the leader of the Christian community in singing its prayer and praise, and the procession is one occasion when a richer embellishment would be welcome, although the participation of the people in the procession itself (rather than spectators) would be encouraged if they were singing while moving along the procession route.

The Stations

The Stations of the Cross provide another occasion for the singing of the congregation. The hymn "At the Cross" is a tradition in many places, and although this song is readily singable, it is one that demands close attention for a proper rendering. The hymn verses that join the various stations together is a meditative song by nature, and a psalm would be of value, particularly Psalm 21; it is long enough, and is the perfect meditation-chant upon the sufferings and triumph of the Christ. There are booklets for the Stations that rely upon Scripture for their inspiration; the use of the 21st Psalm would make a Scripture Service of this popular devotion, and be of great importance in the education, as well as the devotion, of the people.

Novenas

The novenas to the Lord Jesus, the Holy Spirit, or to several of the Lord's saints are services that usually admit of a fixed formula, not only with regard to the prayers, but the hymns at well. Article 13 of the Constitution is actually a mandate for change, for many services contain elements that do not accord with the spirit of the Church's worship. We must await such a revision, but much can be done even now to bring such services into closer approximation to the principles of the liturgy. For example, some elements of existing devotions could be incorporated into Bible Services, so that Scripture and the devotional needs of the people might admit of integration and harmony. The musician can do much to change the impoverished character of certain devotions by the choice of music to be sung. The hymns for certain novenas were chosen at a time when no better hymn was available, and that situation has appreciably changed.

Hymns in praise and worship of God would be used to replace some present novena hymns, and so the correct liturgical emphasis upon our Father as the person to whom the saints address their prayers would be gained. Secondly, the times and seasons of the liturgical year should be taken into account, for the Church year must appear as the framework of all Christian prayers, whether personal or public. Thirdly, hymns in honor of all the saints might be used, but only if they reflect the spirit of liturgical prayer; ideally they would be hymns to God praising him for the wonders he performs through his holy ones, and asking that we be joined to them in sharing his glory. The sung litanies would provide a further possibility for the novena, such as the Gelasian Litany, or perhaps the special form of the Common Prayer that may be in use in a particular diocese. Such a practice would not be difficult, and it would place the needs of the individual within the context of the whole estate of Christ's Church, fulfilling the injunction of Saint Paul who bids us to make supplications "for all men; for kings, and for all in high positions, that we may lead a quiet and peaceful life in all piety and worthy behavior" (1 Tim 2:1-2).

The Sacraments of the Church

Lastly, the musician can be of great help in making the communal nature of the sacraments of the Church more evident, and in the life of the parish this would include Baptism and Confirmation. Since the latter sacrament may now take place within the Mass, this should guide the choice of hymns used for Mass. Hymns to the Holy Trinity, in whose name we are baptised and confirmed, and hymns to the Holy Spirit are eminently suited to public celebrations of the sacraments. The new rite for Confirmation in English allows the people to respond to the versicles sung by the bishop, and to answer their "Amen" to his prayers.

Baptism has already become a parish celebration in many places, and hymns for the congregation heighten this communal aspect of the sacrament. The sacraments appear in practice to be what they are in theory: acts of Christ that are communal, festive prayer, in worship of the Father, whereby men receive the merits of the Savior's redemption, and are made holy.

CHAPTER FIVE

HYMNS AND PSALMS

"We sing a hymn to the Lord's glory with all the warriors of the heavenly army" (Constitution, Art. 8). Within the shortness of this phrase the long history of hymnody is encompassed, and traditions that reach back to Paul are renewed by a pope who bears his name. The "least of the Apostles" encouraged the young Christian community at Colossae to "teach and admonish one another by psalms, hymns and spiritual songs, singing in your hearts to God by his grace" (Col 3:16). It was counsel which the saint himself took to heart, for the Acts of the Apostles narrates how, while in prison, "Paul and Silas were praying, singing the praises of God" (16:25). They were not "praying *and* singing," but their song was itself the prayer, and this is the Catholic attitude towards the nature of a hymn.

In general, hymns are metrical compositions, and usually indicate songs that are not scriptural texts, although there is evidence that some of the phrases used by the New Testament writers were fragments of early Christian hymns and liturgical acclamations. St. Ambrose is usually credited with the development of hymnody in the Western Church, and the Reformation of the sixteenth century is accepted as the age when the vernacular hymn became popular. Since some Protestant groups did not favor the use of any songs save those which were taken from the Bible, there arose the practice of setting the psalms to metrical settings, and many current hymnals include these metrical psalms together with hymns and ancient plain song melodies.

The Value of Hymns

Although the Catholic theory of the hymn as a sung prayer rightly places such songs as forms of divine worship, in practice many of the hymns used by Catholic parishes have not measured up to the spirit and nature of the Church's public prayer. Pius XII, in his encyclical letter *Mediator Dei*, sought to restore the true notion of a hymn in his efforts to renew the Church's liturgy:

> if they are not profane or unbecoming to the sacredness of the place and function and do not spring from a desire to achieve extraordinary and unusual effects, then our churches must admit them, since they can contribute in no small way to the splendor of the sacred ceremonies, can lift the mind to higher things, and can foster true devotion to the soul (No. 50).

In later writings, this same pope noted that hymns "can be a powerful aid in keeping the people from attending the Holy Sacrifice like dumb and idle spectators" (*Musicae Sacrae Disciplina*, No. 64), and can perform the great work of "attracting the Christian people and enlightening them, in imbuing them with sincere piety and filling them with holy joy" (No. 65). Hymns at Mass contribute to the communal spirit, and each voice becomes an actual offering, and a share in the sacramental worship. They have a rare quality of moving men's hearts, in addition to their main purpose of expressing man's praise to God, and are usually easy to remember, enabling us to bring them to mind at will, and thereby enlarging the number of prayers we can use throughout the day.

The Qualities of a Good Hymn

Since congregational hymnody plays such an important role in the worship of the Church, it must possess the holiness, beauty, and goodness of form which the Church demands for her music; hymns must be thoroughly consonant with the Christian celebrations, and encourage an active participation in all the rites and services. In the encyclical letter, *Musicae Sacrae Disciplina*, the qualities that hymns must have are outlined, and the further liturgical and practical suggestions that must be taken into consideration.

They must be in full conformity with the doctrine of the Catholic faith. This prerequisite stems from the very nature of our worship as an expression of faith, whereby all who share the same Baptism gather around the same Lord, with whom they join in worshipping the Father. Hymns actually serve the function of a catechism, for they express the teachings of the faith, and cause it to be remembered to the degree that words and music can impress the mind and heart.

They must also express and explain that faith accurately. The fullness of belief demands this. Sometimes a poetic expression can provide a metaphor of comparison that anchors the doctrine in one's mind, but such terminology can also run the risk of sacrificing something of precision in thought. Many of the hymns that lean heavily upon sentimentality do not accurately explain Catholic teaching, and so are not fitting as Church music.

They must use plain language and simple melody. Here the emphasis is upon the words, for the text must govern the music of a hymn, and both should be simple. The pope added that hymns *must be free from violent and vain excess of words.* Certainly any references to non-Christian concepts should be avoided. In "Mother Dear, O Pray for Me," for example, temptation is described as "pleasure's siren"; the hymn also contains terms that are out of date, and the simplicity of petition is obscured by unintelligible phrasing. Since the English translation used in the Mass has avoided archaic expressions, such as "thee" and "wert," etc., hymns should also be written and revised to conform to the modern idiom of speech wherever this is possible. Nor is it essential that the verses rhyme; many of the most beautiful hymns of the Roman Breviary do not rhyme at all, and the forcing of words into a rhyme scheme leads to artificial inversion, all of which is unnecessary and confusing.

As to simple melody, this is the ideal characteristic of a good hymn for congregational use. It involves several components.

1. *Pitch.* The pitch of most hymns, with the exception of those to be done by a choir, should be lowered to fit the capabilities of a mixed congregation. The normal range is from middle C to the second D above. The range of hymns should therefore extend from B Flat below middle C to the second E above.

2. *Melody.* Awkward and clumsy intervals should be avoided; they are unlovely to begin with, and then only a choir can manage them with any grace. For example, the sixth is an interval that must be used with great care; in "Mother Dear" it is a cause of slow movement, while in

"God Moves in a Mysterious Way," this same interval adds dignity and power.

The movement of the melody is basic to music, and the hymn should avoid chromaticism, and move by diatonic progresson. "O Lord, with Wondrous Mystery" is a hymn that contains scale-wise motion, and is quite effective. It almost carries the singer along. Each phrase is self-contained, and the whole of the hymn presents a flowing effect. Paul Hume has described the desired movement and pairing of intervals as "a certain shapeliness and unity," which is typified in many of the plain chant tunes.

3. *Rhythm*. The rhythm must likewise be simple, and the use of dotted rhythm often results in poor presentation and improper accentuation. Many of the "good, old hymns" are neither "good," nor "old," nor "hymns," and some are actually waltzes! If the hymn does not proceed with movement and freedom, it will move slowly, and will prove a distraction instead of a prayer. A strong accent is needed in order to obtain the correct rate of speed, but every word that falls on a strong beat should not be stressed. The fewer the accents, the more fluent will be the rhythm.

Despite the fact that they are short and easy, they should manifest a religious dignity and seriousness. When hymns are short and easy they serve the purpose of the liturgy best, for then they aid the full participation of the people, and "flow over" into the daily life and thought of the Christian. Easiness refers to their singability, and this is the most desired mark of a hymn. It should be able to be learned within a matter of minutes, first by listening to the choir (preferably) or a cantor sing it through, and then by singing it immediately afterwards. The dignity and seriousness insisted upon is entirely consonant with the high purpose of the liturgy, and is not meant to forbid music of a joyful nature. "Praise God from Whom All Blessings Flow" is an excellent example of a short, easy, and dignified hymn of praise. "Praise We Our God with Joy" is equally majestic, and yet conveys a real spirit of joyful enthusiasm.

In addition to the qualities laid down by Pope Pius XII, there is also the nature of liturgical music to consider. As an expression of Catholic doctrine, hymns should also be indicative of the nature of Catholic worship. Therefore they should not allow of texts that do not reflect a true liturgical perspective. At Christmas, the carol is a tradition among families and nations, and yet some of them should not be sung in church. Christ is the "Eternal Child" of the Father, a term which was frequently used by the early fathers; he is not the "Sweet Babe of Bethlehem," although he was once an infant. The term should be avoided. "O Come and Mourn with Me Awhile" depicts the Virgin as still mourning, and is a sentimental portrait of the anguish that Mary knew, but it is hardly proper to our understanding of the Passion, and the reference to the deriding "Jews" suggests that we not use it in our worship.

Since the text should be indicative of the true nature of the Church's public prayer, it should be objective rather than subjective, and communal rather than individualistic in its outlook. The references to "my Jesus" and "my Mother" are not characteristic of our community worship. Such hymns have often been used in schools to teach the children, and have crept into the singing of hymns during the Mass and other functions. Such poor hymns should be avoided, not only because they are bad in themselves, but also because they do not meet the needs of worship. Now is the time to use proper hymns both in school and in church, in order that future generations may receive a rich heritage of good music.

The subjective element is based upon a false piety, and conveys religious emotions that are exaggerated and unreal; being bad music, even secular music of the eras in which they were written, they are worse prayer. The texts must reflect a proper liturgical attitude, chiefly a Godward direction, and not merely a subjective need. This echoes the thought of Pius XII in demanding that hymns explain the faith accurately, for many of the bad hymns looked upon Christ in his human life, stressing this aspect of the Savior's personality in a familiar manner, and neglecting the work of his salvation, and the Mystery which he is.

How the Hymns Should be Sung

Hymns should require as much practice as any other portion of church music. This is true for the choir as well as for the congregation, and all it demands is a little time and effort, or else we shall be right back to the days when the same hymn is used over and over again.

1. *Primary emphasis upon the words.* The music expresses the meaning of the texts, and the congregation should concentrate upon the meaning of the words more than upon the tune itself. Interpretation is essential to good singing, and this depends upon the principles of good reading. Perhaps the congregation should be asked to merely read aloud and together the words of the hymn to be taught, or listen to them being recited carefully by a lector or cantor.

What should stand out immediately is that the *sense* of the words is brought out by careful grouping of words and phrases, and that a slight stress given to key words is enough to distinguish them. Such subtle emphasis produces the proper result in the singing of plain chant, and should guide hymnody as well. As has been noted, the fewer the accents (and these but slightly stressed) the more flowing will be the presentation of the hymn. Incidentally, the stresses will not always occur in the same places in every verse, so heavy accents should be avoided. The sense of the phrases depends upon the completion of the thought contained, and phrases should be treated in their unity as governed by the words, whenever this is musically possible. The fifth verse of the "Sunday Hymn" should find the first two musical phrases sung as one, in order to complete the thought:

"Holy Spirit, You impart / Gifts of love to every heart."

2. *Contrasts in tone should be avoided.* Expressive singing does not mean changing from soft to loud tones, for these variations are as unwelcome as changes in pace. The theatrical element is out of place in the church, and evenness, but not monotony, is the desired norm.

3. *A variation in musical treatment is desirable.* Congregational singing should be the aim of every choirmaster and pastor, but singing the same melody several times over can be tiring. There is much to commend the practice of choir and people alternating in the singing of a hymn, with the harmony of the choir's music providing enough variety to prevent monotony. Moreover, this practice will also help the people to maintain the correct speed and emphasis, which cannot always be done when the choir and the people

constantly sing together. Vaughan Williams' arrangement for his "Hail Thee, Festival Day!" is a moving piece of music, with men and women alternating portions of each verse.

4. *Excesses in speed should be avoided.* The slow, mournful rate of speed does as little for a hymn as a rate that is too fast. Each hymn usually bears the indication of the tempo in which it should be sung, and this is best observed, as it rests upon experience of many years (at least for the older hymns). Breathing should be an aid to understanding the meaning of the words, and so the principle should be followed that every punctuation mark does not indicate a breath, which usually means a break in time as well.

Simply stated, the words are to be held in greater importance than the musical notes which clothe the text; if the syllables to be accented receive a slight stress, and whole lines are sung in one breath, an even and flowing hymn will result. The meaning will be greatly enhanced when two lines that complete a thought are joined together.

The Psalms

In recent years, much has been done to restore the psalms to the people as their public and personal prayer; the envisioned singing of the psalms at the Introit, Gradual, etc., will make the singing of these scriptural songs an intimate part of their worship. Their great value, apart from the wide range of emotions and thoughts they express, is that they are the very Word of God, which is strong enough to shatter rocks, sensitive enough to pierce to the division between bone and marrow.

The recent revival in psalmody again goes back to Pius

XII, to whom we owe so much for the current liturgical renewal. During his pontificate a new Latin translation of the Psalter appeared, one that was certainly more intelligible than the old. Soon, in 1953, the Gelineau psalm appeared, and eventually several composers presented settings for the psalms which attempted to restore them to congregational use.

There has been much controversy over what setting is best for the psalms, but essentially all argument revolves around one question: Are there good arrangements for the psalms available, which any congregation can readily learn and like? The answer is in the affirmative.

1. They may be set to the eight Gregorian modes. This has been done effectively in many places. There is no discrepancy between English and Gregorian chant when the singing of psalms is concerned, understanding that even the Latin verses demanded allowances for extra syllables. In one Eastern diocese recently, the entire congregation of over 1,000 sang Vespers from the Office of the Dead for their pastor; the psalm tone was very simple, and the effect was hauntingly beautiful and reverent.

2. The Gelineau psalms, with their simple antiphons, have proven their practicality in their English form. The rhythm of the stanzas is based upon stressed syllables occurring regularly, with intervening syllables varying in number. The regular beat is a great help in congregational singing, and the speed is the normal speed used in speech and recitation.

3. Fr. Somerville has written new translations of the psalms, with musical formulae appropriate to the mood of each psalm, working on principles closely allied to that of

the Gregorian psalm tones. Similarly, Sister Mary Paschal, C. PP. S., has adapted several psalms to Gregorian settings, complete with chant-like antiphons, and there are various other attempts at Psalmody in use throughout the country.

Since the psalms enjoy an undisputed primacy over hymns, their use is strongly encouraged, especially during Mass and Bible Devotions. The use of an antiphon with the psalms has a practical feature that is worth noting; they are usually short and easily learned, thus doing away with the necessity of written music when teaching the people.

A problem arises whenever the use of the psalms is discussed, namely that there is a lack of biblical orientation among Catholics. They are not familiar with psalms, and do not understand the references to incidents and ideas that are found elsewhere in the Bible. Some teaching will be necessary if the psalms are to be restored as the prayer of the people. Sermons might treat of the psalms on occasion, and study clubs or discussion groups might undertake a more thorough examination of the meaning and content of these songs. The parish school might consider a more biblically-oriented treatment of the truths of religion, and parish groups could possibly use a psalm as their opening and closing prayer. Whatever devices are used, the results cannot but be beneficial, for the renewal of the liturgy implies a recapturing of the spirit of the psalmists, and an understanding of the Christian significance of the psalms will make the singing of the psalms a fruitful experience.

CHAPTER SIX

THE LEADERS OF CHURCH MUSIC

. . . because it is impossible for the bishop always and everywhere to preside over the whole flock in his church, he cannot do other than establish lesser groupings of the faithful. Among these the parishes, set up locally under a pastor who takes the place of the bishop, are the most important; for in some manner they represent the visible Church constituted throughout the world.

And therefore the liturgical life of the parish and its relationship to the bishop must be fostered theoretically and practically among the faithful and clergy; efforts must also be made to encourage a sense of community within the parish, above all in the common celebration of the Sunday Mass (Constitution, Art. 42).

This Article outlines the scope and procedure of the Sunday Mass program, and presents the ordering of leadership in matters of church music as well. The bishop is the first "leader of music" in a certain sense, for he is the "high priest" of his diocese, "from whom the life in Christ of his faithful is in some way derived and dependent" (Art. 41). As the chief liturgist, he presides over the Eucharistic celebration throughout his diocese, either by himself, or through the pastors and priests he has appointed, and therefore he directs the prayer of the Church, whether recited or sung.

His task is to select the hymnal and list of approved music for the parish, and to choose only good music with consideration given to congregational singing.

Under him, the pastor "who takes the place of the bishop" is the "leader of music" within the individual parish, a role that is one of enforcing the directives of the diocese concerning sacred music, and of enlisting the aid of musically competent directors, organists and members of the choir, among whom we also list the cantor. The success of the entire musical program depends upon the support and enthusiasm of the pastor, and in many cases where the priest is also a musician, the choir and congregation become quite proficient at singing the Mass, since their pastor has an understanding of the problems of the choir director.

The bishop and pastors must be considered leaders if the pastoral direction of the Council is to be realized, and if music is to resume its rightful role in worship, which is always to be done under the presidency of the bishop, and never apart from his directives.

But if the liturgical life of the parish is to be fostered "theoretically and practically," and a "sense of community within the parish, above all in the common celebration of the Sunday Mass" is to be encouraged, then the leaders of church music technically speaking have the prime task of effecting in practice what the Church has commanded be done at Mass. Theirs is a distinct vocation, not only because of God-given talents and the desire to serve the Church, but because the present Council has once again stated the Church's call for help in the task of reform, and extended her welcome to musicians. This definite "call" is a specific clarification of the general call to holiness which every Christian receives, an intensification of which was presented by Pope Paul VI and the Council fathers:

> sacred music is to be considered the more holy in proportion as it is more closely connected with the liturgical action, whether it adds delight to prayer, fosters unity of minds, or confers greater solemnity upon the sacred rites (Constitution, Art. 112).

The role of the musician is one of importance and prominence because of its closeness to the ministry of the altar, and due to the "ministerial function" which music enjoys. To the artist who is "firm in his faith," the late Pope Pius XII addressed a special task and mission:

> The Church has always honored and always will honor this kind of artist. It opens wide the doors of its temples to them because what these people contribute through their art and industry is a welcome and most important help to the Church in carrying out its apostolic ministry more effectively (*Musicae Sacrae Disciplina*, No. 29).

Their usefulness in building the community awareness of the parish will depend upon how well each of them realizes that the renewal of the liturgy begins with their own personal renewal, and with their recognition that the leadership they show to the choir and congregation will eventually lead to an effective Mass program. By the term "leader of church music" is meant the choir director, the organist and the cantor, with each choir-member associating himself with the task of leader of the singing congregation.

I. THE CHOIR DIRECTOR

Ideally, the choir director would be the director of all music within the parish, even within the school, and receive a salary for his full-time duties. This is not feasible in most parishes, but certainly the salary given to a director (and/or organist) should be based not only upon his "industry" but upon his "art" as well, taking into consideration the long years of study. The director of music is an important position in non-Catholic churches; it should be given even greater prominence within the Catholic parish, especially since any underestimation of the well-trained musician is tantamount to a mistaken notion of the importance of the solemn liturgy. The budget for salary and materials should not be relegated to the "incidental" column of the parish ledger! The very notion of minimal pay for considerable work is as much against papal teachings as is the false idea that singing is not really important to the worship of God.

Relationship to the Pastor

The pastor should decide upon the program to be followed in his parish, arranging the schedule for the Sunday High Mass, and the other Masses, which should all be celebrations marked by song. Working with the pastor involves whatever musical ability the choir director can bring to the selection of suitable hymns, from which the priest can select those which conform to the liturgical ideal, for the liturgy is the domain of the parish priest by his office. The ability of the individual parish will be considered as well, for parish differs from parish "as star differs from star in glory" when it comes to singing, and repertoires must be built, and good results maintained. When priest and choir director work together to put into effect the liturgical directives of the diocese, then the program of music is carried out smoothly and effectively.

Relation to the People

Since congregational singing is the first aim of the musical program, with the end in view that choir and people may alternate with each other in singing the Mass, it must be held that the choir director stands in direct relationship to the people in general, and to the choir in particular. He is responsible not only for the selection of music that will enable both to take part, but for the training and directing of both. It has already been stated that each is to sing his part, and only that part, and that the choir is to assume the role of leader; allowing the choir to alternate with the congregation in the singing of the Ordinary, the Council also appears to want the people to join with the specialized singers in chanting the Proper parts of the Mass, (which have been the choir's by custom, but which were listed in the Constitution as parts belonging to the people). The role of the choir—to sing the leading parts; the role of the people—to join with the choir in singing the Ordinary, and the Proper when this is feasible. A typical Sunday Mass program for High Mass might be arranged as follows with respect to the composition and direction of the music. It must be understood, of course, that this outlines only one of many possible arrangements—for example, for the Introit (and other parts of the Proper) the choir and the people can alternate in other ways according to the possibilities of the music.

Before Mass:

Hymn in harmony by the choir, appropriately chosen (or lead the parish rehearsal, if necessary).

Entrance:

> *Ch.* Sing Antiphon of Introit.   *All* Alternate Psalm verses of the Introit until doxology. Then *Ch.* repeats antiphon.

Ch. Alternates "Lord have mercy" with People.

Pr. Intones *Glory to God in the highest.*

Ch. And on earth peace to men of good will.

Ch. We praise you.   *All We bless you. We worship you.   We glorify you. We give you thanks for your great glory.*

Ch. Lord God, heavenly King, God the Father almighty.

All Lord Jesus Christ, the only-begotten Son.

Ch. Lord God, Lamb of God, Son of the Father. You, who take away the sins of the world.

All Have mercy on us.

Ch. You, who take away the sins of the world.

All Receive our prayer.

Ch. You, who sit at the right hand of the Father,

All Have mercy on us.

Ch. For you alone are holy.

All You alone are Lord.

Ch. You alone, O Jesus Christ, are most high,

All With the Holy Spirit, in the glory of God the Father. Amen.

All Answer priest's greeting, reply to Collect.

Service of Word

> *Ch.* Begins Gradual chant.
>
> *All* Repeat *Alleluia* after choir, and again after Versicle. Alternate with choir in singing Creed.

Eucharistic Sacrifice

> *All* Answer greeting of priest.
>
> *Ch.* Sings Offertory Antiphon.   *All* Possibly sing additional verses of Offertory Psalm.   (or)
>
> *Ch.* Sings Offertory Antiphon, and supplementary motet.
>
> *All* Sing replies to versicles before Preface.
>
> *Ch. Holy   Peo. Holy, Holy Lord God of hosts.*
>
> *Ch. Heaven and earth are filled with your glory.*
>
> *All Hosanna in the highest.*
>
> *Ch. Blessed is he who comes in the name of the Lord.*
>
> *All Hosanna in the highest.*
>
> (or people join choir in unison Sanctus.)
>
> *All* Answer *Amen* to Ending of Canon Prayer.

Communion Rite

> *Pr.* Sings "preface" to Lord's Prayer. *Our Father* sung by all.
>
> *All* Sing responses to versicles at Fraction of Host.

Ch. Lamb of God, who take away the sins of the world.

All Have mercy on us. (Third time) *Grant us peace.* (or people join choir in unison Agnus Dei.)

Ch. Sings Communion Antiphon. *Peo.* Alternate with choir in singing psalm verses.

Ch. May sing hymn or motet according to length of the rite of distribution of Holy Communion. Also appropriate for people to sing additional English hymn (or psalm) at this time.

All Reply to Postcommunion, greetings of priest;

Dismissal

All Answer *Thanks be to God* to celebrant's dismissal.

All Sing recessional hymn.

Ch. Sings additional recessional appropriate to Sunday or season.

The same format applies to the Low Mass, with choir taking verses alternately with people (hymns), and singing Processional and Recessional (possibly second hymn at Communion).

The selection of music depends upon the choir-director, and the instruction which he gives his choir. Notice that there are two singing groups, choir and people; the latter group actually means "all," for the term "people" should always refer to the whole body of the faithful, of which priest, choir-director and choir form a part.

Relation to the Choir

This is the group of voices with which the choir director works consistently, and for whom all his energies are expended. He it is who selects them, places them where they will do the most good, trains them properly, and conducts them, achieving balance and precision. He should have three prerequisites:

1. Knowledge of a good repertoire. The choir master alone can gauge the abilities of his choir, and thereby select music that will highlight the strength of certain sections or of the choir as a whole, rather than any weaknesses.

2. Ability to train an amateur choir. The director who knows the "tricks of the trade" saves valuable time in working with the choir, being able both to train new members and to maintain the standards of a group that has been singing for some time.

3. Ability to plan a program well. The music for the entire year should be planned in advance, and the music for any particular Sunday should be introduced long before it is due for rehearsal. Each rehearsal should be prepared for carefully, in much the same way that a teacher prepares for class; the material to be covered should be gone over beforehand, and the techniques of presentation, as well as any foreseen difficulties, handled well in advance of actual rehearsal time. The actual manner of rehearsal and training follows in the next chapter.

II. THE ORGANIST

There is some question as to whether or not the choir master and the organist should be the same person. It is not the purpose of this short work to discuss the weight of either opinion, although a thorough knowledge of the organ is indisputably of value for the director of music. Certainly he should at least be able to play the piano, and know something about registration, and the selection of stops peculiar to the organ used in church.

Relation to the People

Since this musical instrument "is to be held in high esteem," adding "a wonderful splendor to the Church's ceremonies," and powerfully lifting up "man's mind to God and to higher things" (Constitution, Art. 120), it also occupies a high place in being called upon to restore congregational singing to its rightful place, enabling man to lift up his voice, as well as his mind, to God. Pius XII termed the organ "especially fitted to the sacred chants and sacred rites," and giving "an almost heavenly joy" (*Musicae Sacrae Disciplina*, No. 58). The organ is "especially fitted" to aid the congregation as well as the choir in the singing of the Mass.

Although great differences exist between pipe and electronic organs, and even between identical organs installed in different churches, certain basic rules should guide the parish organist in his service of supporting the singing by the body of the faithful.

1. The organ should never dominate the singing, whether the music calls for a solid *"forte"* or a sustaining *"piano."*

2. In supporting and leading the congregation, the tremolo should be ignored.

3. A congregation will respond best to a firm diapason tone (preferably the use of eight-foot stops is recommended) with a solid pedal bass at various times.

4. In addition to this solid tone, the registration of the instrument must be aimed at insuring the greatest clarity, to give a definiteness to the rhythm.

5. Firm, rhythmical playing is the chief support of an untrained group; the hands should be lifted frequently, particularly at the ends of phrases and lines, so that the playing is not *too* smooth.

6. In introducing hymns and chants, a sizable portion of the melody should be played, and not merely a note or two; furthermore, the lines played should complete the sense of the text, otherwise the people will stop at the end of a line instead of proceeding to the second line which completes the thought.

7. The exact speed at which the hymn should be sung must be the rate used in playing the introduction. Since this introduction is a prelude to the hymn, not only the tempo, but the expression as well must characterize the playing. The hymn "Now Praise We All Our God" should not be introduced on soft swell stops, but on a fairly loud great organ (possibly including four-foot diapasons and even reeds); flutes and string in eight-foot and even four-foot combination can add the necessary brightness and fulness for congregational use.

The importance of the fifth rule deserves special attention. Clean, rhythmical playing, not too *legato*, is the best aid to congregational participation. The lifting of the hands from the keys insures this definition, and also aids the people in breathing properly. The secret of getting the people to start in unison is to get them to breathe together prior to the first note. If the introduction is played well, and *at the same tempo* as the hymn demands, all that will be necessary is to lift the hands off the keyboard for one count, then start on the next beat, and maintain the speed of the introduction. Lifting at the end of complete-sense phrases is essential for good breathing, and good breathing is a prerequisite for good singing.

The balance of volume is a difficult thing to judge from the console; if at all possible, the organist should have a competent musician listen from the body of the church, or go down while another plays the organ. Lastly, something should be mentioned about the practice of improvisation. It is best left to only the accomplished organist, and even then there is little need for it. If interludes are used, there is a wealth of good music available, and the choice of music must be governed by the same principles of liturgical appropriateness that govern the selection of hymns.

One further matter needs to be discussed, and that is the necessity of starting the music promptly. The Introit should be begun before the sacred ministers appear, so that the music is really an accompaniment to the procession. When the Sanctus is to be sung, the words "Holy, Holy, Holy" should appear as a continuation of the preceding Preface, and not as a separate musical hymn that follows an interlude. The organist should not wait until the celebrant has started to recite the Sanctus or Agnus Dei before playing.

Relation to the Choir

Whereas the organ leads and sustains the congregation, its main function as far as the choir is concerned is to supply instrumental background. Harmonized singing by the choir should be accompanied by softer stops, preferably without the pedals. At times, there should be no accompaniment for the choir, which brings out the true tone of the blended voices; if accompaniment is used, then the registration should take into account not only the voices singing, but the character of the music as well. Certain norms for accompanying the choir are generally recognized as acceptable, and should prove helpful.

1. A good organ technique demands that the notes of a chord be pressed simultaneously, and released in the same manner.

2. Eight-foot stops are to be preferred in accompanying the vocal sounds of choir, or choir and congregation. Reeds, mixtures, twelfths and sixteen-foot stops are best ignored for use with a choir, and used sparingly (if ever) for leading the congregation.

3. Do not always couple your manuals.

4. Play the notes for the pedal as written, and not an octave lower, as all too often happens. Pedal stops are also to be played with both feet, just as both hands are used for the manuals; in other words, all the pedals are to be used, and not just the lower part of the pedal board.

5. The organist should always be aware of the primary place of importance that is given to the text, not only when accompanying the congregation, but when playing for the

choir as well. This does not mean a constant changing of stops to convey the right expression for each phrase, but some change, certainly, when the words demand a variation. Avoid any extremes in changing the registration, neither changing too often, nor refusing to change at all.

As every organ is different, no detailed suggestions can be given concerning what stop changes to make, or what technique to follow; only the skilled organist can know how best to use the instrument with which he works and is familiar. Two observations remain, merely by way of repetition.

1. The use of pedals is essential to good hymn-singing, and congregational song. The good organist is well versed in the technique, and knows when to use the pedal board, and when not to use it.

2. The organ should ordinarily be played *legato*; for good congregational singing, the lifting of the hands from the keys will aid the breathing, emphasize the accent, and thereby avoid the temptation to "drag" the melodies.

The Liturgical Use of the Organ

Every church musician is familiar with the directives that govern the use of the organ, and it will be sufficient here merely to recall them.

1. Concerning the Church Year.
    a. The use of the organ is ordinarily prohibited during Advent and Lent, when the Masses are ferial (purple vestments), except when it is necessary to accompany the singing. The exceptions are on *Gaudete* Sunday and Christmas Eve during Advent, and on *Laetare* Sunday in Lent.

b. The organ is forbidden during the Sacred Triduum, from the Gloria of Thursday of the Lord's Supper, until the intonation of that same hymn during the Mass of the Easter Vigil. The organist is expected to play a full organ prelude for about a minute, during which time the bells of the church are rung.

c. It is forbidden during Masses of Requiem, unless needed to sustain the singing. Since the Paschal character of funerals will be brought out by the revision of the liturgical books, it hoped that the use of the organ will be permitted broader scope.

2. Concerning the Organ at Mass.

a. The organ should be played:

1) before Mass, to set the tone for the feast being celebrated;

2) to accompany the singing;

3) during times when the celebrant is not speaking aloud (e.g., during the Offertory and the three prayers before Communion);

4) never during the Canon, a rule often violated by an organ interlude after the Consecration;

5) after the Last Blessing (where a hymn is the ideal).

b. The use of the organ helps in achieving appreciation of the liturgy:

1) by selection of music appropriate to celebration of Sunday or feast (joyful on feasts, etc.)

2) by adding solemnity to special occasions, as the solemn entry of a bishop, etc.;

3) by adhering to the rule that when singing ceases the organ becomes silent.

III.   THE CANTOR

Any effective program of participation requires that the congregation receive not only instruction in how to sing, but actual direction of the singing; this role of "Leader of the Congregation" is the proper realm of the cantor, who is, by definition, one trained in the techniques of leading the community in their song. Untrained people cannot be expected to do well in fulfilling their function within the community unless they are aided by one who is well-versed in music and the ability to direct a singing group.

His role is essentially one of helping the choir to perform *its* task of leading the people; he is an extension of the choir, as it were. Ideally, the choir should occupy a prominent place in the church, where they can exercise their role effectively, in which case the choir-director might serve as the cantor, or leader of the people's song. Actually, some other person, acting in harmony with the choir-master, is recommended, and the congregation would learn to follow only his direction. Otherwise, they would be looking at the choir director throughout the whole of the service. It seems best, therefore, that the people have a leader of their own for their constant leadership.

What Does the Cantor Do?

Realizing that the ideal cannot always be achieved, and that many churches are arranged at present so as to exclude the choir from a prominent place (although there is no reason why they could not occupy the front pews of one section, even though the choir-loft is built over the front entrance), the cantor will have two tasks: first, he is to lead the people, having first given them instructions, and be located in front of them; secondly, he is to make sure that the people "keep up" with the choir, maintaining the pace which the choir sets, and joining in at the proper time when alternating with the choir. In short, the cantor brings the people into the closest possible union with the sacred action of the Mass, joining their voice to that of the choir in a unified worship.

Suggestions for the Cantor

In almost every diocese, the services of men are utilized to lead the congregations in singing the Mass, or in singing hymns that parallel the Proper chants. In order that their specific function be practical and uniform, the following aids are recommended.

1. When leading the people he should be visible from all points of the church, preferably located to the side, rather than directly in front of the altar. This will insure effective leadership, without calling attention away from the celebrant.

2. He should know something about the use of a microphone, which is an invaluable aid. He can therefore use a quiet, reverent voice when giving directions, such as page numbers, etc., and yet present enough volume to lead the actual singing.

3. When giving directions, invitations, (or even giving a commentary, when this practice is used and the roles of cantor and commentator are combined) the cantor should use only short, pithy phrases, precise and to the point.

4. Before Mass, even though all are not present, the can-

tor should make use of the time to prepare the people:

    a) by telling them the page numbers and titles for the hymns to be sung;

    b) by getting them to speak together in unison, paying attention to the meaningful expression of words (rehearsing the recited parts of the Low Mass Program, for example);

    c) by correcting possible flaws noticed over the course of several repetitions of a hymn, and by going over difficult passages;

    d) by leading the people in learning a new hymn.

This "warm up" period before Mass is recommended no matter how skilled the congregation may have proved itself. It does not take long, if handled carefully and with skill, and after a while the leader of the people's song will be able to gauge his time accurately, and use it more effectively. In addition, the time spent is worth weeks of effort when one considers the enthusiasm and encouragement it engenders.

    5. During Mass, the cantor will aid the participation:

    a) (if there is no separate commentator) in a non-musical way by giving directions for sitting, standing, etc., using slight gestures of the hand. The cantor may substitute for the choir on occasions when it is not present by leading in litanies, psalm verses, etc.;

    b) by using movements of the hand that are large enough to be clearly visible to all;

    c) by keeping his eye upon the choir-master, since the cantor is doing his task, and that of the choir, partially;

    d) by not overpowering the congregation with his

own singing, increasing the volume of his voice only when necessary to prevent the congregation from falling apart, sliding, etc.

The cantor serves an important function in the community, especially in making the parish aware that it *is* a community; he works with the choir, and is perhaps the director (when the choir is seated in the body of the church, visible to all) or a member; but above all, he enjoys an office of his own, that of directly leading the People of God in their worshipful singing of His perfect praise.

CHAPTER SEVEN

THE AMERICAN PARISH SCENE

"Choirs must be diligently promoted," states the Constitution on the Sacred Liturgy (Art. 114). And why? Because the liturgical rites receive "a more noble form when the divine offices are celebrated solemnly in song, with the assistance of sacred ministers and the active participation of the people," (Art. 113). The choir lends this note of solemnity, and even more importantly, makes the active participation of the people possible.

As regards the full and conscious participation of all the faithful, the choir is essential, its primary role being the *musical leadership and education of the christian assembly at Mass*. It supports the congregation in the singing of the Ordinary, and fittingly renders the Proper of the Mass, since the congregation could not be expected to sing these chants without rehearsal and training. The participation by the people in singing the Proper chants has received encouragement from the Constitution, as has been noted, but in practice such a participation will be confined to responsorial chanting, or the singing of a given refrain. The solution to the problem of combining the efforts of choir and people lies in alternating portions of the music between both groups, one form of which has already been outlined.

As regards the solemnity of the sung celebration, the

role of the choir is paramount. By the careful singing of the Proper chants, and by the skilful rendering of motets, antiphons, etc., they embellish the setting of divine worship, thereby giving the people an example to follow, instead of relegating them to a passive role. Both duties of the choir demand the perfection of the choir itself, and the training of voices for the fitting rendering of sacred song. If good music is to be insisted upon, then no less must we insist upon its proper execution by a good choir; good music sung well is the only liturgical music, and for this a choir is needed.

Building the Parish Choir

Only when the role of the choir is properly understood and appreciated can the choir director hope to obtain recruits for his group, and provide them with enthusiasm for the training that he must impart to them. Needless to say, the formation of a choir in any parish must be carefully planned in advance, with plenty of advance "publicity" before the actual establishment of the group, and plenty of support from the pulpit of the church. Not that a sermon on the necessity of a choir should replace the homily of the Mass, but certainly within the course of the homily itself, or in a well worded announcement, the function of the choir can be discussed and a plea for co-operation made.

A good campaign of telephoning, visiting, etc., is to follow up the introductory notice, and possible candidates should be told clearly what is expected of them in time spent in rehearsing, actual performance, etc. Once the obligations of a choir are definitely known, members are in a better position to make their decision. In any case, the problem of organizing a choir will present the same difficulties as ever, but they will be increasingly less troublesome if the choir enjoys a proper understanding of its important service within the liturgy, and the support and encouragement of the entire parish, priests and people.

What to Look for in a Choir Member

The minimum requirement for a choir member is the ability to learn by ear, to sing a melody exactly as one hears it being sung. The perfect choir member is one who can sight-read, and is acquainted with the musical staff and its notation thoroughly, possibly through previous training with a musical instrument. The person who has had some voice training is not necessarily the best choice for a choir in the ordinary parish, unless that person will be of assistance in training the choir vocally; otherwise he (or she) might not fit in too well with the unexperienced voices. There will always be one person, at least, with some experience at solo work, and such a man might be chosen to do the work of the cantor, the only "soloist" other than the celebrant that is either allowed or desired by the liturgy.

Usually the choir-master will not be able to do much choosing from among trained singers, but will be more than happy to find people who are willing and eager to help out, and who have a good speaking voice. These people will develop with training and practice. A voice that is not coarse and raspy will be the best material for the average parish, and if the person has a voice of ordinary quality and power but a good ear, he will be far better suited to sing in a group than the person who has a strong voice but a weak ear.

Auditions for the Choir

Years of experience with singing groups have convinced most directors of the need for auditions, and even though the term might frighten prospective choir-members, the director can certainly explain the need for some type of testing in order to place them in the proper group, etc. They should feel that the audition is important, but they should not expect the audition to assume the proportions of try-outs for the opera. A simple procedure can be adopted that will assure both member and director of the quality and correct placement of the voice. Several methods are available, each following a basic technique, suggestions for which are listed here.

1. Hold the auditions in some place other than the church, preferably in a small room used for rehearsals.

2. Use the piano, and never the organ.

3. Take each candidate individually; when dealing with a boys' choir, take them collectively first. This puts them at ease and eliminates the nervousness that is only natural to their age.

4. Have the candidates sing a scale to a chosen vowel sound ("ah," or "oh," etc.) and raise the scale a tone higher each time.

5. Test the ear; have the candidate sing various notes as soon as they are struck on the piano. This may be done to whatever pattern proves most useful.

6. Select a standard hymn, with soft accompaniment only; this will indicate whatever peculiarities might go unnoticed in merely singing notes at random.

7. Several tests enable the choir-master to find out how

well the prospective singer is able to find the note for his part. For instance, have the person sing the lower of two notes struck simultaneously, or the middle of three notes sounded together. These short tests provide a wealth of information, and should be used, together with many other tests available.

8. Give a reading test first, to determine the ability of the singer to express himself adequately. The text of a well-known hymn, and then of a hymn that is not common, would form a good basis for judging the expressiveness of the person being auditioned.

In every audition, as in every practice session, the main virtues of the choir-master will be his patience and sympathetic approach, essential qualities if the choir will ever be taught to sing with ease and naturalness.

The Training of the Choir

Rehearsals

The success of a good choir depends upon how well the time for practice is employed, and how well the training is remembered from the time of practice until the actual performance of the music of the Mass. There are no specific regulations set down, and each parish will choose a different time for rehearsal, but it is universally accepted that evenings are the best time, when the mind is more at ease and receptive. Many suggest that the rehearsal be held as close to Sunday evening as possible, which is Friday in most cases, although one parish encountered plans its rehearsals for Monday night—the director explains that the mistakes of Sunday are clearer and can be effectively treated the following day. A date later in the week is generally held to be the most advantageous time, although such non-musical considerations as shopping-night, evening devotions, etc., will have to be taken into consideration. Every rehearsal, however, should be characterized by certain familiar aids. They include:

1. The weekly rehearsal should be from one and a half to two hours in length, with some rests (and humorous observations) to create the proper atmosphere.

2. A minimum of twenty minutes should be allowed as a "warm-up" before the Sunday Mass.

3. Rehearsal must begin on time. The friendly exchange of conversation should take place after the session, not before, and late-comers are best ignored and allowed to take their place, without calling attention to their tardiness or interrupting the procedure.

4. Each rehearsal begins with prayer, and sung prayer is recommended as an excellent method of teaching a new hymn.

5. The prayer should be followed by breathing and vocalizing exercises for at least five to ten minutes. If the opening hymn is sung after such exercises from time to time, the effect of the exercises will become immediately apparent to the group.

6. The director should know what music is to be covered, and in what order, long before the working-session begins.

7. The room for the rehearsal should be other than the body of the church (or the choir-loft), well lighted and airy, with the music readily available.

8. The piano should be used, as it is of greater service in giving the precise pitch and in helping those members who are unable to sight read. When occasion demands, the choir

can move to the church proper to try out the effect of combining organ and voices, although this will not be required too often.

9. Needless repetition should be avoided. If difficult intervals are pointed out beforehand, many errors can be eliminated, and much time saved.

Training the Voice

The ideal situation would be one in which the choir director was also a voice teacher, since the development of a beautiful tone is his aim, and the primacy of the words of the sung prayer demands a careful articulation and expression. If at all possible, the director should enlist the help of a qualified voice teacher for part of some rehearsals, and work with him in training certain individuals outside the time of rehearsals if such is needed. In many cases this will not be feasible, and most of the training will fall to the choir master directly, and he should be acquainted with the basic principles of training the human voice. Such principles will be used throughout practice sessions whenever a difficult passage is attempted, or whenever the interpretation and expression of the words call for special attention.

Tone

The production of a beautiful tone is the preliminary to all good singing, and it implies an *easy, natural* singing that appears to be effortless. Tone is characterized as a sound whose pitch and quality are well defined as distinct from a diffused sound or noise. As such it is essential to all good singing, and the choirmaster will be asked to concentrate upon the four properties which assure the quality of sound.

1. *Pitch*. The ability to place a note in relation to another is indispensable to the choir member, and functionally more important than the rare gift of being able to identify a musical sound by name, or sing it at will (referred to as 'absolute pitch'). The maintaining of a good pitch involves one of the most basic principles of good choral singing, namely that *the choir member is as much a listener as he is a singer*, and the hearing of the proper tones is an invaluable aid in obtaining a good quality of sound. There are numerous exercises that can be used to insure correct pitch, but all of them are intended to produce the same results— the full use of every resonating cavity, the co-ordination of breathing and voice apparatus, and the ability to sing in an easy, relaxed manner.

Flat singing may be due to poor ventilation, which is why an airy room is recommended for rehearsals. Other causes may be laziness (in some cases) and overwork—this latter cause may often be remedied by periods of relaxation.

Sharp singing is usually the result of anxiety, or improper breathing and the consequent "forcing" of the voices. If such a situation arises, the director would do well to tone down the volume considerably, so that *all* the singing is *piano* or *pianissimo*. The proper volume can be corrected later on without any difficulty.

2. *Duration*. The second element to tone is the actual length of each note. In maintaining the correct speed, the habit of individual time-keeping cannot be insisted upon enough, for it is a good device to firm, rhythmical singing.

The choir must take care to avoid either dragging or hurrying. Both of these can be avoided if instrumental accompaniment is dispensed with for a continuous period covering several rehearsals. One helpful exercise is the singing of a hymn, with alternate verses being sung *pianissimo* and *forte* while care is taken not to vary the speed. The common faults of going too slowly, or too fast, are usually allied to the softness or loudness of the piece respectively.

3. *Intensity*. The first rule for assuring the proper shading is the principle that the *use of the imagination is paramount in expression*, which, after all, is the result of emotional feeling. If the singer can understand that the emotions of love, joy, sorrow and peace can be expressed by the music alone, he will be able to express the text with greater definition.

Again, the ability of the choir to *listen* will be helpful, for *crescendos* and *diminuendos* occur when the singers listen carefully for them, and understand that they demand greater practice than one might expect. One sure way of guaranteeing a correct, dynamic expression is to follow the rule: *crescendo* means "begin to think of loudness," and *diminuendo* means "begin to think of softness," and that both movements of increasing and decreasing the volume have their moments of climax. Thus every crescendo should be begun softly, and *every* voice must contribute to the full effect. However, the use of exaggerated changes in volume is to be avoided as not proper for liturgical music, and needed only for the fitting execution of the music as it was written.

4. *Tone color* (timbre). This refers to the peculiar quality given to a tone by particular voices. By such quality, notes of the same pitch and volume are distinguished. The

tone color to be achieved will depend upon the proper use of breathing, precise articulation of vowels and consonants, etc.

Breathing

The foundation of all good singing is correct breathing, which demands firm control. Singing requires a different type of inhaling and exhaling than does ordinary speaking, and breathing exercises should be employed at the start of each rehearsal and performance (during the warm-up session). Two principles might be remembered by the choir-member: 1) the vowels actually carry the tone in singing, and are longer than spoken vowels; 2) far better control is demanded of the singer than of the speaker, and certain methods should be used to arrive at the proper breath-control. Here are a few suggestions:

1. Stand erect, but relaxed; the hands might be held behind the back, a posture that any age group will use with benefit.

2. The throat must be loose and open.

3. The shoulders should *not* be raised.

4. It must be remembered that in singing breath is taken through the mouth.

5. In singing, a long breath is taken in, and exhaled as the singer wishes.

6. Pay careful attention to the expansion of the lower ribs. Take a deep breath, hold it for a few seconds, and exhale very slowly and steadily. Audible counting will be helpful.

7. Avoid any tightening of the throat, and by no means attempt to hold the breath at the throat, but rather *at the waist*.

8. Do not over-tax the lung capacity. A full breath is not demanded for each musical phrase to be sung; common sense and experience will dictate the amount of air to be inhaled.

Many books about music and voice-training contain useful exercises from which the choir director may choose.

Attack

Insufficient attention to attack (and "release") is the cause of lack of definition, and even poor timing. Attack refers to the beginning of a passage or phrase with precision and clarity, and release implies the reverse. One principle to remember in dealing with attack, is that *the phrase begins with the intake of breath.* Consequently, the taking in of the breath must be moved by the same emotions which are encouraged by the text of the phrase.

A second maxim that is useful states that the mouth is to be shaped for the initial sound *as the breath is drawn in,* and not afterwards.

Enunciation

The greatest effort must be placed upon the vowel as the foundation of a good tone, but perfect singing demands that *every vowel and consonant receive equal attention.* Many teachers of music choose a different starting point to acquire an even flow of sound on all vowels; some use "oo" or "ah," while others insist upon "ee" or "ay." Both groups should be used, since they counteract each other. It is best not to train on one type of vowel sound to the exclusion of others. Common sense dictates that the vowels used in actual singing be employed equally for practice. When any vowel sound is to be used in vocalizing exercises, *it should first be conceived mentally* before being sung, and all "forcing" of the voice is to be avoided. A few points should receive attention.

1. Attack the vowel, which actually makes the tone, *at the same time* as the consonant.

2. Some vowels are simple, others compound; when compound vowels (those having more than one sound) are being sung, the principal tone should be sustained. The word "how" really combines two sounds: "ah" and "oo"; it should be sung "h-AH-oo."

3. The purer the vowel sound the richer the tone.

4. The vocal consonants, especially "m" and "n" should be considered as tone-carriers.

5. The shaping of the lips is important, and each vowel requires its own peculiar shaping of the lips, to be pronounced accurately.

6. Bad pronunciation of consonants is the cause of any "roughness" in attack, and initial and final consonants are to be enunciated with great clarity.

Balance

In harmonized singing, the first principle is that the parts should be evenly balanced in power, which means that everything is to be scaled to the weakest group (generally the alto). In this respect, only by listening can the choir achieve balance if the weakest part is to produce as much tone as is possible.

The work of balance demands much care and attention to detail. The principles of this have been treated in many manuals for directors of music.

Blend

It is important for each choir member to realize that he or she is a part of a group, not apart from it, and that effective choral work necessitates that no one voice should stand out from the group within the choir, nor from the ensemble of voices that forms a choir. The perfect blending of voices depends upon two points: 1) a uniform production of tone, and 2) the identical shaping of vowels. One method of assuring blend involves the selection of a hymn, or unison chant, to be sung through softly by each part in several different ways: humming the tune with lips closed and then parted, and using various vowel-sounds, with the vowels being sung in an easy manner (perhaps with each person smiling).

Sight Reading

One last item to be covered is the training in reading music at sight, a talent that is extremely helpful. For instance, much of the inability to make a good "start" is due to the fact that singers are unable to think the first group of notes; the same is true when difficult intervals are encountered. If the passages could be recognized as similar to, or different from, passages already learned they can be carried out with little difficulty, and sight-reading can accomplish this.

The easiest method is the Tonic Sol-Fa system, which is adequately discussed in many manuals (cf. bibliography).

Building the Singing Congregation

There are many additional points to be considered in training the parish choir which it is not the purpose of this short book to discuss. The importance of a well-trained group cannot be stressed sufficiently, not only for the performance of their own role within the Mass, but for the proper carrying out of the role which the Constitution on the Sacred Liturgy wishes to emphasize. Active participation of the people seems to be the *cantus firmus* of the Constitution, and the minute detail given to the rites and ceremonies appears as an exercise in counterpoint. In working to achieve the artistic, prayerful participation in sacred song by the sacred People of God, there are two types of situation that present themselves. The first is the ideal situation where the parish is blessed with a good choir, and the second is where no such tradition exists, and the congregation is forced to work without a choir (such as a small parish, a chapel in a resort area, etc.).

Where there is a choir

Simply stated, the problems of congregational singing are almost solved where there is a choir, and if the choir sings the congregation's part, and all the responses together with the people (instead of singing them in place of the people), then the problems are completely solved. The congregation needs the assistance of the choir so that, as one writer puts it, "their part may be really a part and not an apology." Everything that has been written so far concerning the use of hymns applies here to congregational singing, and the choice of good, stirring hymns can be the best incentive for any congregation (to witness the enthusiastic response to "Holy God," despite its overuse).

The first point of consideration is the time for rehearsals. Two possibilities are apparent.

1. *The "warm-up" session before the Sunday Mass, which is a practical aid before every Mass in which hymns and psalms play a large part, and an essential aid for the High Mass.* The amount of time will vary from parish to parish, as the schedules for the Masses will not always

allow for a definite, universally acceptable period of time; a maximum of 10 minutes might be chosen, and the people should be encouraged to be present. The first rehearsals will treat the responses, and progress to the more difficult music. When the rehearsal before Mass begins with a sung prayer, the hymn learned on the previous Sunday will be of use here, in addition to the fact that further singing will make the hymn familiar. The responses, no matter how well they are known, should be the first item; they are short, and give the congregation the encouragement they need. Next, the shorter chants, such as the "Lord have mercy," and portions of the Gloria or Agnus Dei. Lastly, the opening hymn (processional) or verses to the Introit could be rehearsed, leading into the celebration proper.

2. *A parish rehearsal, perhaps following Vespers or some other evening service.* A definite amount of time (perhaps 20 minutes at first) should be settled upon, so that the people will know what to expect. The music to be covered will be determined by the selections made for the following Sunday, and this rehearsal is the perfect time to introduce new music. However, familiar music should be given to the congregation, for it will be difficult enough to get some congregations to sing in the first place without needlessly confusing them with too much new music. Certain special occasions, such as the great feasts (Holy Week and Easter, Christmas) and parish functions (Dedication, Confirmation) will necessitate parish rehearsals, and these should be taken into account by the pastor when arranging for them.

The presence of the choir at such rehearsals, apart from the time spent before Mass, is essential, and will insure the best results. The congregation will be moved to sing, and the choir will appreciate its own proper role more clearly. If the parish rehearsal falls on the same night as the choir rehearsal, they could be combined for part of the time, although what has been written concerning a separate room for choir rehearsals still applies.

During the celebration of the liturgical rites, a number of people strategically located will form a "fifth column," as it were, a hidden choir to bolster up the efforts of the congregation. Certain individuals could be chosen for this task (even those who could not make the choir because of "no room"), but groups within the parish, such as the sodality, Altar society, etc., could fulfill this function.

This point leads to another—the use of hymns, responses and chants as the opening prayers for parish meetings. This is surely a simple way to train the people in at least one hymn, if not more. The various groups will welcome a fuller role in the greatest spiritual endeavor of the parish—the communal celebration of the Eucharist.

The hymnal used in Church should be the basic text for music in the schools, for the school in any parish is actually a school in being a parishioner, and this involves the worship of God primarily. A greater use of the school music program should be the normal procedure, for the present liturgical revival will be the commonplace for generations yet to come, not in the sense that it will lose any of its vitality, but in the sense that the people of the future will be thoroughly familiar with the patterns of worship with which we are now becoming familiar.

When the choir and people rehearse together, and if time allows, the choir should sing the hymn or chant by themselves before singing it with the people. A third singing of the hymn by the people alone might occasionally be used to test the ability of the congregation to learn music, and to let them realize that, although they need the leadership of the choir, they must not sacrifice their own participation by letting the choir do all the work. Moreover, the singing of the hymn by the choir will enable the congregation to imitate the correct speed and expression desired.

Where no choir exists

In those parishes in which it will be impractical to have a choir, the role of the choir will be taken by the cantor, for certainly each parish can provide at least one man who can perform this task. He will act in the same capacity as the choir during rehearsals by singing the hymn through, by supporting the singing of the people with his own voice (amplified through the use of a microphone, preferably), and encourage the full participation of the people. At Mass he will *be* the choir, singing the Proper parts if he cannot arrange to have them sung by a small group acting as a *schola*, leading the congregation, and alternating with them in certain Ordinary portions.

The choir-less parish will depend upon the various groups within the parish, more so than the parish that has a choir. These people might be seated together, or throughout the congregation, as the need dictates, and if the parish has a school, or gives religious instruction, these children can support the singing of the Mass. For all intents and purposes, if High Masses are sung during the week it would be desirable to have a cantor, or a group of children, selected to do the singing; certainly somebody *other than the organist*, or we will be right back where we started, with an impoverished notion of the communal nature of the sung Mass. Ideally, High Masses should not be arranged unless the people will be present, and trained, to sing the Mass, with at least the cantor performing the Proper parts.

The Use of the Schools

An intelligent program of musical participation demands that better use be made of our schools than has been the case in the past, and certainly this applies to the religious instruction given to the children of public schools. For the future, the instruction in singing the Mass given today will form generations that will live the liturgy, and be familiar with its workings.

1. *The parochial school.* Music should be a part of any well-integrated curriculum, especially in the grammar school. The first recommendation to be made is the adoption of the hymnal used in the diocese (and consequently the parish) as the song-book for school. Many of the music books contain hymns that are not fitting for liturgical use, but which are nevertheless used in Church; some of them are poor music, and even poorer prayer, and cannot convey the right attitude of congregational singing that the children should have. Since a good hymnal will contain some simple hymns, the lower grades should make use of the hymnal as well.

Every school day should begin (and end) with a sung prayer, which affords an excellent opportunity for practicing the music for the Sunday Mass. The hymns used for the Low Mass program can form the concluding prayer, and simple chants, such as the Kyrie or Agnus Dei could be used as the opening prayer of the day by most, if not all, of the classes. The higher grades could rehearse the Gloria and the Creed in their music classes, and the entire school can gather for a short time each week to practice the responses and the Sanctus which should be the most powerful chant of the Mass, coming as it does at the beginning of the Canon, and focusing our minds on the liturgy of heaven.

Since First Fridays are a part of Catholic school life in some places, and daily Mass the center of the day in other places, the Mass should be arranged so that all the children may attend. The hour for Mass might be set at about 11:00 A.M., so that the entire school might be present; such a convenient time will allow the children to have breakfast and lunch at the proper times without discouraging holy Communion, and will also be a better time for singing, when the voices are somewhat more relaxed than at early morning. The week before the First Friday could see practice of all the sung prayers taken from the Mass, and a group of students from the upper grades could take the Proper parts, since the choir will most likely not be able to attend.

The Lenten season will take on its proper perspective of a preparation for the great feast of the Resurrection if the children are being prepared to take part *fully* in the services of Holy Week, especially the Easter Vigil. Their attendance at this "most wonderful night" could be placed within the framework of their sacrifices, and would certainly deepen the awareness of the Paschal Mystery as the center of the parish's life in Christ. In some parishes, daily Mass is not made available to the school children at a convenient time during Lent, since, it is argued, there would then be "no sacrifice" involved on the part of the children. It is hoped that such thinking will give way to the desire of the Church to have each Mass a true celebration of the entire parish. The Lenten liturgy is particularly instructive and meaningful, a "course in Christianity" to prepare us to renew the spirit of our Baptism, and the simple settings of the Mass will move the people to a greater understanding of true repentance and to the notion of our prayers and hymns as "a sacrifice of praise."

The importance of liturgical music should be thoroughly insisted upon in our schools, over and above the necessary training in secular music; otherwise the school is falling short of its purpose, to enable the student to live his religion —and the source of that life is the sacred liturgy. Religion classes, as well as the day itself, could be used for training the children in the music of the liturgy by the use of "sung prayer," for the class day is usually tightly organized, and the teaching of music will suffer if it is "squeezed in" among other subjects.

Nevertheless, although the school-room provides the locale for learning the music of the liturgy, the actual singing must never appear to be a mere performance. Neither must it be seen as a class-room exercise only, but great care must be taken to teach the children that the singing is prayer, and is a part of the parish worship, albeit in a restricted sense.

The individual teacher will select the manual that is best suited to the needs of her class, but the teaching of liturgical music should be the first concern. The different grades might be encouraged to assist at the parish Mass for a given week, and to sing the Ordinary with the rest of the congregation, and the Proper, if there is no cantor. This will divide the labor evenly, and certainly provide the incentive necessary. It must be borne in mind that the vernacular liturgy will demand a re-education of the entire people, and that progress will have to be made slowly at first. The school children will not suffer from the disadvantage of being "too old" to learn, and the success of the parish program of divine worship will largely depend upon how well the children are made to fit into the pattern of participation in each parish.

2. *The C.C.D. instruction classes.* Although not too much time can be allotted for the religious instruction of children attending the public schools, everything possible should be done to give these children the attitude that they are not second-rate Catholics. Even though the hour or so each week presents a challenge to the teacher in "covering the material," a certain portion of each class should be devoted to the practice of hymns and Mass-chants. The idea that they are needed by the Church to make her worship, and their lives, meaningful will prove a good incentive to attendance at the services of the Church, and full participation in the Eucharistic liturgy. Each class should begin and end with sung prayer, and this should be a hymn and at least one Mass-chant. The liturgy itself, if rightly celebrated, will provide instruction, a point that cannot be overlooked, and which should be put to use. Only a few minutes out of each class will do much to create a sense of being appreciated and needed by the parish, of being truly a part of the parish, and will be worth hours of instruction that could not achieve the same results as well.

In general, then, every resource should be tapped, every

possibility examined, such as inter-parish meetings when the music of the Mass, and the hymns, could be rehearsed and sung together, possibly closing with the Holy Mass or a Bible Service. Every meeting of parish groups, every Communion breakfast, every class in school, and every opportunity that presents itself should be used to the fullest in teaching the music of the Mass, that the Mass might be lived in the way that music is sung—beautifully, according to the mind of its composer, and with feeling—for the purpose of sacred music "is the glory of God and the sanctification of the faithful" (Constitution, Art. 112).

APPENDIX

The following list of hymns is given as an indication of the way some of the more familiar present-day hymns can be used liturgically. Other possibilities will suggest themselves to the organist and the choir director, such as an appropriate hymn for First Communion, weddings, visit of the bishop, etc. These hymns are listed according to the feast or season to which they are particularly suited, with a suggestion as to their use during the Low Mass.

HYMNS AND FEAST OR SEASON	MASS
Advent	
Behold a virgin bearing him	Entrance
Behold the Bridegroom cometh	Entrance
Christ the Word to earth descended	Communion
Humbly we adore thee	Offertory
O come, O come, Emanuel	Entrance
O Lord of light, who made the stars	
On Jordan's bank	
The coming of our God	
Wake, awake, the night is dying	Recessional
Where love and charity prevail	Offertory
Christmas	
A great and mighty wonder	Recessional
Good Christian men, rejoice	Entrance
Let all together praise our God	Recessional

O come, all ye faithful	Communion
Unto us is born a son	Recessional
Virgin-born, we bow before thee	

Epiphany

As with gladness men of old	Offertory
Bethlehem! of noblest cities	Thanksgiving
Praise to the Lord	Entrance
Songs of thankfulness and praise	Recessional
The people who in darkness dwelt	

Lent and Passiontide

Accept, O Father, in thy love	Offertory
All glory, laud and honor	Processional
All praise to Thee	Entrance
Draw near, O Lord, our God	Entrance
Look with mercy, Lord	
Lord, who throughout these forty days	Entrance
O Lord who showed us	Offertory
O Sacred Head, surrounded	Offertory
Praise to the Holiest in the height	Recessional
Sing, my tongue, of warfare ended	
This is our accepted time	Offertory

Easter

Accept Almighty Father	Offertory
At the Lamb's high feast	Communion
Be joyful, Mary, heavenly queen	Entrance
Christ be with me	Recessional
Christ the Lord is risen today	Entrance
Jesus Christ is risen today	Entrance
O sons and daughters	Communion

Singers, sing, and trumpets, play	Entrance
The Lord is my true Shepherd	Communion
Ye sons and daughters, let us sing	Entrance
Ye watchers and ye holy ones	Recessional

Pentecost

Again the slowly circling year	Entrance
Come, Holy Ghost, Creator blest	Offertory
Holy Spirit, Lord of light	Offertory
Into our hearts, O Spirit, come	Entrance
O Holy Spirit, come to us	Offertory
To God Almighty we confess	Entrance

Trinity

All hail, adored Trinity	Recessional
Blessed be our God and Father	Recessional
God Father, praise and glory	Recessional
Holy, holy, holy Lord	Recessional
Most ancient of all mysteries	Recessional
Praise God from whom all blessings flow	Recessional
Praise we our God with joy	Entrance
Sunday hymn	Entrance

Feasts of Our Lord

Ascension hymn	Entrance
Bread of heaven, on thee we feed (Corpus Christi)	Communion
Begin, my tongue (Corpus Christi)	Communion
Christ be with me	Recessional
Crown him with many crowns (Christ the King)	Recessional

Hail, Redeemer, King divine	Entrance
(Christ the King)	
Heart of Christ, we sing thy praises	Entrance
(Sacred Heart)	
Humbly we adore thee	Communion
(Corpus Christi)	
Lord, who at thy first Eucharist didst pray	Communion
(Corpus Christi)	
O holy Lord, by all adored	Entrance
Sing, my tongue, the mystery holy	Communion
To Jesus Christ, our sovereign King	Recessional
(Christ the King)	
To Jesus holy	Entrance
(Christ the King)	

Blessed Virgin Mary

Hail, thou star of ocean	Entrance
Hail, holy queen, enthroned above	Entrance
(Assumption)	
Holy Mary, now we crown you	
(May Crowning)	
Immaculate Mary	Recessional
(Immaculate Conception)	
Sing of Mary, pure and lowly	
(Immaculate Conception)	
The God whom earth and sea and sky	Entrance

Miscellaneous

Accept, O Father, in thy love	Offertory
Christians, sound the name that saved us	Recessional
(Holy Name Sundays)	

Father, see thy children (All Souls)	Offertory
Father, we thank thee	Communion
O Father, thou whose hand	Recessional
O God, our refuge and our strength	Recessional
On this day, the first of days	Entrance
To the name that brings salvation (Holy Name Sundays)	Entrance

Benediction

Behold a virgin bearing him	Exposition
Bread of heaven, on thee we feed	Exposition
Christ the Word to earth descended	Recessional
Holy God, we praise thy name	Recessional
Humbly we adore thee	Exposition
O bread of angels	Exposition
O Lord, with wondrous mystery	Recessional
Praise the Lord, all ye nations	Recessional

Weddings

Lord, who at thy first eucharist	Communion
Now joined by God	Recessional
Praise to the Lord	Processional
Psalms 99 or 126 (Gelineau)	Processional
Wedding Psalm 127	Offertory

BIBLIOGRAPHY

The following bibliography is limited to providing background reading for the ideas expressed in this text. A review of the index of any of the periodicals listed will reveal many pertinent articles. The addresses of some music publishers have been provided rather than a list of recommended music because of the present state of flux in this field. A short note to any one of them will bring the reader into contact with an assortment of good, singable music.

ANDREWS, CARROLL T. *A New Organ Method*. Toledo, Ohio: Gregorian Institute, 1959 [G 775].*

APEL, WILLI. *Gregorian Chant*. Bloomington, Indiana: Indiana University Press, 1958.

BERNIER, CONRAD. *Organ Method*. Toledo, Ohio: Gregorian Institute, 1961 [G 912].

DAVISON, ARCHIBALD. *Choral Conducting*. Cambridge, Mass.: Harvard University Press, 1940.

FELLEHER, KARL. *The History of Catholic Church Music*. Baltimore, Md.: Helicon Press, 1961.

GELINEAU, S.J., JOSEPH. *Voices and Instruments in Christian Worship*. Translated by Clifford Howell. Collegeville, Minn.: Liturgical Press, 1964.

GRAVES, RICHARD M. *Singing for Amateurs*. New York: Oxford University Press, 1954.

GREGORIAN INSTITUTE STAFF. *Home Study Courses in Harmony,* two and three part counterpoint and Gregorian

* The number listed last in brackets is the item's Gregorian Institute catalogue number.

127

Chant accompaniment. Toledo, Ohio: Gregorian Institute, 1962.

HAGGARD, LARA. *Tone Syllables.* Delaware Water Gap, Pennsylvania: Shawnee Press.

HUME, PAUL. *Catholic Church Music.* New York: Dodd, Mead & Co., 1956.

MCNASPY, S.J., CLEMENT J. "The Sacral in Liturgical Music" in MCMANUS, FREDERICK R. (ed.) *Revival of the Liturgy.* New York: Herder & Herder, 1963.

MURRAY, O.S.B., DOM GREGORY. *Music and Liturgy.* Bath: Downside Abbey.

NICHOLSON, O.S.B., DOM DAVID. *Vernacular and Music in the Missions.* Cincinnati, Ohio: World Library of Sacred Music, 1962.

PELOQUIN, C. ALEXANDER. *Choral Precision.* Toledo, Ohio: Gregorian Institute, 1962 [G 953 for SATB choirs; G 954 SSAA choirs; G 966 TTB choirs].

PETERS, FLOR. *Little Organ Book.* Boston, Mass.: McLaughlin & Reilly, cf. Introduction.

Periodicals

Caecila, 3558 Cass St., Omaha, Nebraska.

Catholic Choirmaster, Holling Press, 501 Washington St., Buffalo, New York.

Diapason, 2010 International Building, Rockefeller Center, 630 5th Ave., New York, N. Y.

Musart, National Catholic Music Educators Association (N.C.M.E.A.), 620 Michigan Ave., Washington 17, D.C.

Proceedings of the Annual Liturgical Weeks. Washington, D.C.: The Liturgical Conference, 1950-1964.

Proceedings of the Workshop on Music Methods, edited by

Dr. Richard Werder. Washington, D.C.: Catholic University Press, 1950-1963.

Worship, St. John's Abbey, Collegeville, Minnesota.

Papal Statements

The Constitution on the Sacred Liturgy of the Second Vatican Council and the Motu Proprio of Pope Paul VI. With a commentary by Gerard S. Sloyan. Glen Rock, N.J.: Paulist Press, 1964.

Divini Cultus, Apostolic Constitution of His Holiness, Pope Pius XI, from "The Popes and Church Music." Conception, Mo.: Conception Abbey Press, 1956; and Washington, D.C.: National Catholic Welfare Conference, 1964.

Mediator Dei. Encyclical Letter of His Holiness Pope Pius XII on the Sacred Liturgy. Washington, D.C.: National Catholic Welfare Conference.

Motu Proprio on Sacred Music (1903) by Pope St. Pius X. Toledo, Ohio: Gregorian Institute, 1950; and St. Meinrad, Indiana: Grail Publications, 1960.

Musicae Sacrae Disciplina (On Sacred Music). Encyclical Letter of His Holiness Pope Pius XII. Washington, D.C.: National Catholic Welfare Conference.

Sacred Music and the Sacred Liturgy. Instruction of the Sacred Congregation of Rites, September 3, 1958. Washington, D.C.: National Catholic Welfare Conference.

Music Publishers

Hymnals, choir music, and other participation aids may be secured from the following firms:

Gregorian Institute, 2132 Jefferson Ave., Toledo, Ohio.

McLaughlin & Reilly, 252 Huntington Ave., Boston, Mass.

World Library of Sacred Music, 1846 Westward Ave., Cincinnati, Ohio.

Mass Cards and Recordings

In addition to the Mass Card published in conjunction with the Parish Worship Program, many other types, including those for Forty Hours Devotion, are available from the music publishers listed above. The same publishers can supply recordings of various Mass programs.

Liturgy

Church musicians interested in achieving a better understanding of liturgical doctrine and practice may consult the following books:

DALMAIS, O.P., IRENÉE. *Introduction to the Liturgy.* Baltimore, Md.: Helicon Press, 1961.

DAVIS, S.J., CHARLES. *Liturgy and Doctrine.* New York: Sheed & Ward, 1960.

DIEKMANN, O.S.B., GODFREY L. *Come, Let Us Worship.* Baltimore, Md.: Helicon Press, 1961.

HOVDA, ROBERT W. (ed.) *Sunday Morning Crisis.* Baltimore, Md.: Helicon Press, 1963.

LITURGICAL CONFERENCE. *Priest's Guide to Parish Worship.* Distributed by Helicon Press, Baltimore, Md., 1964.

MILLER, C.S.C., JOHN H. *Signs of Transformation in Christ.* Englewood Cliffs, N.J.: Prentice-Hall, 1963.

REINHOLD, H. A. *Bringing the Mass to the People.* Baltimore, Md.: Helicon Press, 1960.

SLOYAN, GERARD S. *The Liturgy in Focus.* New York: Paulist Deus, 1964.